The Name Book

A book about our surnames, Christian or given
names, and nicknames. Plus an insider's list of
people who've changed their names, and a section
on people who've entered the language as words.
With a useful guide to pronouncing difficult names,
and hundreds more facts about names. A book that
really tells you 'what's in a name'!

The **One Hour Wordpower** *series*

WORD BANK
Expanding Your Vocabulary
WORD CHECK
Using Words Correctly
GOOD GRAMMAR IN ONE HOUR
THE NAME BOOK
THE SECRETS OF SPEED READING
GUIDE TO WORDPLAY AND WORD GAMES
CRISP CLEAR WRITING IN ONE HOUR
SPELL CHECK
1000 Most Misspelled Words

One Hour Wordpower

The Name Book

GRAHAM KING

Mandarin
in association with
The Sunday Times

A Mandarin Paperback
THE NAME BOOK

First published in Great Britain 1993
by Mandarin Paperbacks
an imprint of Reed Consumer Books Ltd
Michelin House, 81 Fulham Road, London SW3 6RB
and Auckland, Melbourne, Singapore and Toronto

Copyright © Graham King 1993
The right of Graham King to be identified
as the author of these works has been asserted
in accordance with the Copyright, Designs
and Patents Act 1988

A CIP catalogue record for this title
is available from the British Library
ISBN 0 7493 1524 5

Printed and bound in Great Britain
by Cox & Wyman Ltd, Reading, Berks

This book is sold subject to the condition
that it shall not, by way of trade or otherwise,
be lent, resold, hired out, or otherwise circulated
without the publisher's prior consent in any form
of binding or cover other than that in which
it is published and without a similar condition
including this condition being imposed
on the subsequent purchaser.

Contents

Acknowledgements

The author wishes to pay tribute to the
formidable mountain of name information
made available by genealogical researchers both
in Britain and in the US.

Readers who wish to learn more about names
are invited to consult any of the books
recommended in the Reading Guide.

Introduction

After an hour with this book you'll never need ask, as Shakespeare did, 'What's in a name?', although here we're talking about Rose the person, not the flower.

There is quite a lot wrapped up in our names; in some cases a history stretching back a couple of thousand years. There are Normans and Vikings, Romans and Celts, romance and bloodshed, Puritan piety and Hollywood glamour.

Names dominate our lives. While most of us get by quite comfortably with a vocabulary of several thousand words, our stock of names – those we use and those we store in our memories – might add up to between 50,000 and 100,000. Every time we meet someone, visit a place, use a new product, watch a TV programme, listen to a pop song or read a book, we are adding to our already huge reservoir of names. And all the time our vocabulary of everyday words, for most of our adult lives, remains fairly static.

So it's worth taking a look at our names. This book deals only with the names of people, beginning with our surnames, then our first or given names, followed by other interesting things about names: fashions and popularity, unusual, funny and embarrassing names, why people change their names, nicknames, and names of people that we now use as words.

Although *The Name Book*, like the others in the *One Hour Wordpower* series, is designed to be consumed in a short time, you will almost certainly discover that it is also a valuable reference work on human names. But as there are around ten billion of us in the world, the names under discussion are necessarily restricted to those you'll most likely come across in English-speaking countries.

Although *The Name Book* is above all dependably

authoritative, it is leavened along the way with many fascinating – and hilarious – insights into the curious verbal appendages we call our names.

What's In A Surname?

Think of a name. Any name. No matter how outlandish your invention, it is very likely that someone, somewhere, will be known by that name.

When people have names like Hannah Hollyhock, Mary Puddenfoot, Robert Terrible, Shlomo Turtledove, Serious Misconduct and Ginger Screws Casanova – believe it or not, these are or were the real names of real people – you can see that names are like grains of sand: they are as uncountable as they are unaccountable.

On the other hand, your name may be, well, rather homely; in fact, excruciatingly plain and common. In most English-speaking countries the top ten most widespread names don't vary much. Over the past decade or two, here are the most common names in Britain and the US:

	UNITED KINGDOM	UNITED STATES
1	Smith	Smith
2	Jones	Johnson
3	Williams	Williams
4	Brown	Brown
5	Taylor	Jones
6	Davies	Miller
7	Evans	Davis
8	Thomas	Wilson
9	Roberts	Anderson
10	Johnson	Taylor

Depending upon the country or region, the Browns, Jones's, Whites and Greens may move up a place or two. In New York City, Cohen occupies fifth place and Rodriguez tenth, reflecting its large Jewish and Hispanic populations. Lee is the seventh most common name in the Manhattan telephone directory, which may be because many Lees are Chinese. But, wherever you go in the English-speaking world, Smith is invariably the front-runner, a fact that can produce identity crises for a good many of them. In Wales, recently, two couples arrived at the Babbacombe Hotel, near Newport. The first couple stood before the reception desk and the man sheepishly gave their names. 'I don't expect you'll believe this, but we really are Mr and Mrs Smith.' The man behind him stepped forward, his face growing redder by the second. 'Excuse me,' he said to the manageress, 'But *we* are Mr and Mrs Smith!' 'Don't worry,' the manageress said soothingly, 'I'm Miss Smith.'

But if the Smiths think they have problems, how about the Zhangs in China? There are one hundred million of them, making Zhang the world's most common surname, although according to the *Peking Daily* there might be even more Wangs than Zhangs, with Lui or Li not far behind. Chosen names are also limited to a few fashionable or 'lucky' names, so that it has become a national problem that so many name combinations are the same. Consequently, people are assigned nicknames like 'Big', 'Little' or 'Old'. In a Shenyang factory, where ten employees were named Li Wei, they were distinguished as Long-Haired Li Wei, Big-Eyed Li Wei and so forth.

This was pretty much the situation in England in Anglo-Saxon times, when no surnames existed at all. Without family names, people were known by their first (and only) names; when the population increased and this became confusing, nicknames were tacked on as an aid to identification. The brash and adventurous Eric became Eric the Modig, or Bold; while red-haired Eric was called Eric the Red. In time both nicknames evolved into surnames, so centuries later our Erics became Eric Mudie and Eric Read respectively. The process received a stimulus after 1066 when the Norman conquerors stipulated that all first or given

10

names were to be drawn from an official list of saints; because of the restricted choice and the subsequent duplication, surnames, or family names, became the norm – no pun intended.

Many of today's surnames, of course, do not have this Anglo-Saxon, Norman or medieval ancestry, but most have nevertheless been passed down through many generations and, at the same time, have spread all over the world. Even a recent surname, coined for example when a family arrived from Eastern Europe in the 1930s and changed its name from Breitenberger to Brite, is now at least three generations old.

Surnames are an important part of the English language (they frequently become quite common words, as you will discover later) and it is both useful and fun to know something about them, their origin and meaning. Here is a necessarily brief list of some of the more common surnames, including, perhaps, your own.

Ackerman	*Aecermann*, an Anglo-Saxon farmer
Ackland	Anglo-Saxons who lived in or near oak forests. A William de Acklane is recorded in the thirteenth century
Adam	From the Hebrew first name, meaning 'man'
Agnew	From the Norman French *agneau* = lamb; nickname for a meek person
Ansell	*Ansehelm*, Anglo-Saxon for 'sacred helmet'
Archer	A bowman, from Saxon times
Arlott	A nickname for a young rascal
Baldwin	A teutonic Christian name, meaning 'brave friend'
Ball	(Also Ballard) Old Norse *böllr* = short, fat person
Bannister	*Banastre*, French for basket maker
Barber	Up until Henry VIII, a surgeon-barber

Barclay	(Also Berkeley) A Roger de Berchelai was known in the eleventh century, but could have originated from families living in Berkeley, Glos, or Berkley, Somerset
Barker	Either from bark, used for tanning, or from *berchier*, French for shepherd; both thirteenth century
Barraclough	Family from the lost Yorkshire town of Barraclough
Barrett	*Barrette*, French for cap-maker, the trade of a Norman family which settled in Ireland
Bassett	Like the hound; originally a nickname like 'Shorty' for a small man
Bates	Shortened from Bartholomew, in turn a boatman
Beadle	(Also Biddle, Buddle, Beadell and Beedle) From the Saxon *bydel*, later beadle, a parish official
Bean	(Also Been) Nickname for a happy, pleasant person
Beaumont	(Also Belmont) Possibly ancestors of Rogerius de Belmont, or of families attached to the thirteenth-century estate, Beaumont-Le-Roger
Bellamy	Norman French *bel ami* = fair friend
Benson	With Benn and Bennett, this surname springs from the Latin name *Benedictus*, a popular first name in the twelfth century
Best	*Beste*, medieval English for beast and in turn an unkind nickname for someone hard and cruel
Biggs	(Also Bigg, Begg) From the Middle English *bigge* = big and strong
Blake	A fairly recent surname of Irish origin, from a term describing a dark-complexioned person

Bone	From the Old French *bon* = good
Bowen	This can be traced to Madoc Ap Oweyn, who lived in Wales in the late thirteenth century
Boyd	Scots and Gaelic nickname for 'yellow-haired' but could also derive from the Isle of Bute
Boyle	Although an ancient Irish nickname for 'fair-haired', many Boyles could claim ancestry to the Englishman Richard Boyle who became the Earl of Cork; his son Robert invented the compressed air pump
Brady	(Also Brodie) May be descendants of Michael de Brothie of Morayshire, Scotland
Bruce	From a place-name in Norman France; several knights named Bruce accompanied William the Conqueror
Buchan	Descendant of Richard de Buchan (thirteenth century) or from families living at Buchan, Aberdeenshire
Burgess	*Bureis*, French for a freeman of the town
Burke	From Burgh, Suffolk, and from William de Burgo, who settled in Ireland and became Earl of Ulster, which is how it became an Irish name
Burns	In Old English, burn and bourne meant a stream; someone who lived near a stream
Cahill	Cathal, an early Gaelic warrior
Callaghan	Descendants of the tenth-century Celtic King of Munster
Cameron	Camshron, or 'hooked nose' identifies the highland clan, while the lowland clan originated from Cameron in Fifeshire in the thirteenth century

Multiple identity

If you have ever had trouble remembering the names of guests at a party, you would have enjoyed attending the party thrown by London gallery owner Peter Johnson in 1990. Providing, however, your name was also Peter Johnson, for the invitees were exclusively men with the same name, namely, Peter Johnson. In all, twenty Peter Johnsons attended, and introducing everybody must have been either hilarious or monotonous. The wine waiter, the only one present who wasn't Peter Johnson, had no trouble remembering the names of all the guests.

Campbell	*Caimbel*, Gaelic for 'crooked mouth', a nickname
Carroll	(Also O'Carroll) A mainly Tipperary tribal name that can be traced back almost a thousand years to Cearbhal and his son O'Cearbhaill
Carson	Scots name of uncertain origin, but from the fifteenth century
Cartwright	Maker of carts, dating back to the thirteenth century
Casey	*Caisin*, Gaelic for 'crooked one'
Chalker	Families living in the chalk Downs of Southern England
Chamberlain	A steward of a manor and later of royal households
Chambers	A tax collector, nicknamed after the *chambre*, or room, in which the taxes were paid
Chance	A man over-fond of gambling
Chapman	*Ceapmann*, Anglo-Saxon for a travelling salesman
Child	*Cild*, Anglo-Saxon name for the youngest in a family

Clarkson	Son of a clerk
Collins	A family from the south of England which settled in Ireland
Conner	*Cunnere*, a medieval inspector of ale
Constable	An ancient derivation from the Latin *comes stabuli* which evolved into the office of a person in charge and then, in the fourteenth century, into the local constable. As a surname it dates from the twelfth century
Cook	In Anglo-Saxon times, *coc*, or a pieman, first recorded as a surname (Aelfsige Coc) in the tenth century
Cruikshank	Scots nickname for a bowlegged person
Cunningham	Originally *Cunegan* in the twelfth century, most probably from a Scottish place-name
Curtis	From the Old French *courtois* = well bred
Cutler	A maker of or dealer in cutlery
Daly	Descendants of the honourable thirteenth-century Baron O'Dalaigh of County Westmeath, Ireland
Daniels	A Hebrew name that was transplanted to Wales
Darwin	Old French *deor wine* = dear friend
Davies	(Also Davey) Transposed from the Welsh forename David from as far back as the twelfth century
Day	A maid or servant
Dempster	Deemer, a judge
Dennison	(Also Denison, Denson) 'Son of Denis', a common forename derived from the third-century St Denis of Paris
Doolittle	Whether it was a nickname for an idler is not known, but the surname dates from the thirteenth century

Douglas	Either descendants of twelfth-century William de Duglas, or from families living in Douglas, Lanarkshire, Scotland
Doyle	A descendant of *Dubhghall*, an Irish description of a 'dark stranger' recorded in the tenth century
Draper	Seller of cloth
Drummond	From the thirteenth-century Scottish baron Malcolm de Drumond
Duncan	A name made famous by Shakespeare. The eleventh-century grandson of Malcolm II, son of Kenneth
Dunn	(Also Dunne) From the Gaelic *d'oun* = dark, brown

Coining names of numbers

Farthing, Penny, Shilling and Pound are not uncommon surnames. And occasionally you might come across a Twelves or a Twelvetrees, or, less often, an Eighteen or a Twentyman. But a Mr One? A Mrs Two? Or Three, Four or Five? Whereas in France you will find the occasional *Deux*, *Cinq*, *Huit* and *Dix* used as surnames, in Britain, for some reason, there is a curious dearth of 'number names'. While Moneypenny narrowly qualifies, 007 unfortunately doesn't count.

Earl	*Eorl*, Anglo-Saxon for a victor, or winner
East	(Also Easton) Someone from the east, or someone living in the east part of a town or district
Eastman	Norman version of *Eastmund* = grace, protection
Eaton	From one of the various English places called Eaton

Edmondson	Son of Edmund, the defender
Edwards	*Eadweard*, Anglo-Saxon for 'guard of property', a surname that drifted into Wales in the fifteenth century
Ellis	(Also Elkin) A pet name shortened from Elizabeth
English	Early Britons who defied the invading Danes and Normans were derisively labelled 'English' by their conquerors
Evans	Evan's son – common because Evan was the Welsh equivalent of John
Fagg	*Facg*, Saxon for a high-class baker. A Clanvagg is recorded in fourteenth-century Kent, and Fagg is still a common name in that county
Fairfax	Fair of hair. Most surnames with the prefix 'fair' probably derive from a descriptive nickname, as with:
Fairweather	Fair of temperament; a sunny disposition
Farmer	*Firmarius*, a collector of taxes, is one derivation but some surnames are likely to have originated from the rural variety
Ferguson	Son of Fergus, a Scottish surname although of ancient Irish origin
Fields	(Also Field, Fielder) Feld is Early English for field; the thirteenth-century James atte Feld may have owned fields or lived by cultivation
Fitzgerald	Son of Gerald, a Germanic name that arrived in Ireland via the Anglo-Normans
Fitzpatrick	Unlike Fitzgerald, an early Gaelic family, probably of noble status
Fletcher	*Flechier*, French for an arrow maker
Flynn	Flann, the red-haired one; thence his

17

son O'Flainn, and then, over the centuries, to Flynn

Forbes Probably descendants of the thirteenth-century Duncan de Forbeys of Aberdeenshire. Also Scots Gaelic for a field

---

Children of the workhouse

It was not unusual, in Victorian times, for newborn babies to be left by their distraught unmarried mothers on the doorsteps of workhouses and foundling hospitals. Nor was it unusual for such babies to be given off-the-cuff surnames like Midnight, Monday or March, prompted by the time, day or month of their arrival. In one instance, according to parish records, an abandoned baby was found with a half-penny coin gripped in its little hand. The child was promptly given the surname Halfpenny.

Gallacher (Also Irish form Gallagher) Anglicised form of *Gael* meaning servant

Garnett *Grandrium*, Latin for granary; also *gernier* in Old French and garner in English indicate the person owned or supervised a granary

Gentle *Gentil* is medieval English for cultured and the name dates from around the twelfth century

Gibson Son of Gibb, a shortened version of Gilbert

Gladwin Old English first name meaning 'shining friend'

Glanville This family name originated from Glanville in France, via Norfolk

Godwin	(Also Goodwin, Godson, Goodson) Originally an Anglo-Saxon first name, sometimes shortened to Gode: thus Gode-son, eventually Godson
Goldberg	(And possibly such variations as Gold, Gould, Goldbaum, Goldberger, Goldblat, Goldfarber, Goldfinger, Goldblum, Goldstein, etc) Old English for someone with blonde hair but chiefly used for someone working in gold.
Goodchild	God-child; a Goodchilde existed in the fourteenth century
Goodfellow	From the Middle English nickname *gode-felawe*
Goodman	Godmann, Anglo-Saxon for master of the household
Goodwin	Originally a first name meaning 'good friend'
Gordon	Descendants of the Gorduns that existed in twelfth-century Berwickshire
Grant	(Also Grand) From the Latin *grandis* = important
Grenfell	(Also Grenville) Descendants of families from Granville in France via Yorkshire
Griffiths	Derived from the ancient Welsh names *Griph* and *Grufudd*
Gulliver	*Goulafre*, or glutton; there was a William Gulafra living in eleventh-century Suffolk
Hall	*Heall*, in Anglo-Saxon a servant of the manor house
Hamilton	From a Leicestershire place-name, from which descendants moved to Scotland in the thirteenth century
Hampshire	Descendants of Thomas Hamshere,

	originally from the county of Hampshire
Hanson	Son of Hann, the Flemish equivalent of John
Hardy	From the Middle English *hardi* = tough, daring
Harris	(Also Harries and Harry) Derived from 'son of Henry'. The surname was used in Wales from the fifteenth century
Hastings	Descendants of the Anglo-Saxon ruler Hastang
Hayward	Ancient name for a man who guarded a hayfield
Healey	(Also Heley, Ely) Families from Ely, Cambridgeshire. An early example was eleventh-century Huna de Ely
Hobson	(Also Hopkins) Son of Hobb, a variation of Rob, short for Robert
Hodson	Son of Odo, an old Norman name
Hoffman	Germanic nickname for a farmer-landowner
Hope	Families living in one of several old English settlements called Hope, although there are other obscure derivations
Howell	(Also Howells) Derived either from the Breton Huwel, the Old Welsh Houel, or from the tenth-century King Huwal of Wales
Hulme	Descendants of thirteenth-century Geoffrey de Hulm of Lancashire
Humphries	*Hunfrid*, Teutonic for head of the household
Hunt	*Hunta*, Anglo-Saxon for huntsman
Ingham	*Engaigne* is Old French for a confidence trickster, although whether or not twelfth-century Richard Ingaine was one is unrecorded

Huws, Hughes, Howes and Hewes

These and other variations form one of the largest groups of Welsh surnames, yet they all derive from a single ancient Teutonic forename – Hugo. With the coming of the Normans and the canonisation of St Hugonis of Avalon, Bishop of Lincoln, it became equally popular for forenames and surnames – so popular, in fact, that variations became necessary. The Welsh branch almost certainly sprang from the sixteenth-century North Welshman, Ap Hughe.

Ingram	(Also Ingrams) An early Yorkshire name with obscure Teutonic origins
Innes	Descendants from a thirteenth-century Grampians barony
Jackson	Son of Jack, an alternative to John
Jacobson	(Also Jacobi, Jacoby) Not necessarily of Jewish origin; Jacob was a popular pre-Norman name
James	An old name, but not as old as Jacomus or Jacques, from whence it sprang
Jenner	*Engineor*, an old French term for an engineer, may have supplied the origin for this name via the surname Ginnur
Jobson	Son of Job, an old Hebrew name
Joyce	As Joss, a Norman name transported to Ireland
Keene	(Also Keen) *Cene*, Anglo-Saxon for brave; subsequently Kene
Kelly	Descendants of the wild Irish chief Ceallach
Kemp	*Cempa*, Anglo-Saxon for an athlete
Kennedy	Descendants of Ceinneidgh of Glenmora

Kerr	(Scots version of Carr) Old English for someone who lived near a marsh
Kidd	(Also Kidder, Kidson) Derived from Kit or Kitt, short for Christopher
King	From the Old English nickname *cyning* for a leader or for someone haughty or pretentious
Kitson	From the nickname *Kytte*, used for a husband and wife named Christopher and Katherine
Knight	*Cniht*, an Anglo-Saxon page and esquire who became a soldier
Knowles	Southern English nickname for people who lived in the mountains
Lang	Old nickname for a lanky or tall person
Last	Name for the tradesmen who made the lasts, or shoe shapes, for shoemakers
Lawless	*Laghles*, Anglo-Saxon for law breaker
Leach	*Laece*, Anglo-Saxon for a physician
Leslie	Descendants of thirteenth-century Scot Robert de Leslie
Lightfoot	Old nickname for messenger
Livingston	(Also Livingstone) Descendants of the thirteenth-century West Lothian family of Levingestoune
Lloyd	From the Welsh *llwyd* = grey, or grey-haired. Floyd is considered to be the English form
Lynch	The Irish branch are descendants of Loingseach of Thomond and Sligo, while the English branch may derive its name from the Anglo-Saxon for hill-dweller
Lyon	From a family that came from Lyon, France

From Llewelyn to Lewis and other Welsh surnames

The use of hereditary or family surnames is a relatively recent phenomenon in Wales, dating from around 1600; even then, the practice spread both slowly and cautiously, so that just a handful of names dominates all others: Evans, Hughes, Rees, Griffiths, Owens, Pugh, Davies, Jones, Thomas and Williams – all instantly recognisable as Welsh although they were undoubtedly English names originally. The two Welsh surnames that most people know best are Llewelyn and Lloyd, both with the unmistakable Ll. There are also thousands of families named Lewis, which is a shortened form of Llewelyn.

Maitland	*Maltalent*, French for bad-mannered
Marks	(Also Marcus and Marx) From the first name Mark or the German form *Markus*
Marshall	(Also Maskell) *Mareschal*, French for a farrier
Martin	From the forename Martinus, in turn from Mars
Masterson	Son of a master tradesman. An early example is John Maisterson of York who in the fourteenth century was apprenticed to his father
Matheson	From *Mathi*, a shortened version of Matthew

Sir Edward Maufe

There is a wonderful story told about the architect Sir Edward Maufe (MAUFE : *Mage*, Anglo-Saxon for a relative through marriage) who arrived late for a very formal society dinner. Crouching down, he crept up behind the host, sitting at the head of the table. 'I am so terrible sorry,' he apologised. 'I'm Maufe.' The host spun around in surprise. 'But, my dear chap,' he exclaimed. 'You've only just arrived!'

Mayer	(Also Meyer, Myer) From the English Mayor, but more commonly from the Old German
Mayhew	Pronounce Matthew in French, and you have the French connection for this surname
Mellor	Descendants of fourteenth-century Richard de Meluer of Mellor, Lancashire
Meredith	Descendants of Welshman Mereduht Ap Grifin
Merryweather	*Myrige*, Anglo-Saxon for merry, led to the name Muriweder in the thirteenth century, and Merryweather today
Miles	*Miles*, Latin for soldier
Milligan	(Also Mulligan) Mael, a Celtic term for a bald man
Mitchell	From the Hebrew-derived Christian name Michael
Montague	Widespread descendants of families from Montaigu, France
Montgomery	Montgomeri and Mungumeri were two

	versions of this surname, originating from France, in the twelfth century
Moody	(Also Mudie) *Modig*, an ancient term for boldness
Morgan	As *Morgunn* and *Morcant* ('dwellers near the sea'), the name goes back into Celtic antiquity
Morris	A Welsh name deriving from the Latin *Mauritius*, meaning 'the dark one'
Mulligan	See Milligan

Murphy

It's a law; it's a potato; in America, it's a fold-away bed. It's also a sprawling Irish tribe that centuries ago sprang from the sod of County Wexford. One of its earliest members, recorded as living in the twelfth century, was Domhnall Dal Ua Murchadha. The name will never die; certainly not while Murphysborough, Illinois, remains on the map.

Munro	(Also Monro, Monroe, Munrow) From the Gaelic *mur-rotha* = mouth of the River Rotha or Roe

Mac and Mc

Mac is simply 'the son of', and many Scottish surnames evolved from tacking the prefix on to a parent's name, as with the son of Alexander calling himself McAlexander, now commonly McAllister. Sometimes the prefix would be attached to the father's trade or calling; one that survives is MacParson, better known as Macpherson.

Murray	Probably descendants from families living in Moray, Scotland
Nash	Invariably, names incorporating ash derive from families who lived in one of the many places associated with ash trees – Ashwood, Ashton, Ashford, Monash, Saltash, etc
Neil	(Also Neill, Neilson) Scottish version of the Irish forms Neal and Neale, originally deriving from the Norman meaning 'champion'
Nelson	Son of Nell, the feminine version of Niall
Newman	Old nickname for someone settling in a community
Nichols	(Also Nicholson, Nicholas, Nixon) From the common first name Nicholas
Norman	Northernman and Norseman – people who lived in the north
Opie	Cornish, from the medieval diminutive Oppy, from Osbert or Osborne
Palmer	Palmers were pilgrims who returned from the Holy Land, identified by the palm leaves they carried
Pengelly	(Also Pengelley, Pengilly, etc) From ancient Cornish *pen-kelly* = above the wood
Penhaligon	From a place-name near Bodmin in Cornwall
Penrose	From Cornish place-names meaning 'above the heath'
Perkins	(Also Parkin) Derived from the family nickname Peterkin, or 'Little Peter'

Onamia

In Britain, O-names have long been dominated by the Irish O' surnames, led by long columns of O'Briens and supported by the O'Flahertys, O'Haras, O'Sullivans and their kind, with the sullen groups of Olivers and Osbornes, Oakleys and Olsens, Oswalds and Ottleys utterly impotent to do anything much about it. But now the beleagured non-O's have found new allies from West Africa, so that the Ogunyanwos and Obasekis and Obejekomahs jostle for the high ground with the O'Malleys and O'Learys. While the origins and meanings of these exotic new names no doubt offer a fascinating field of study, this book is, we regret, not the place to explore it. But something should be said about the Irish surnames, of which at least one is represented in every street in the land. The O' prefix to a surname indicates grandson (Mac, as in Scotland, denotes the son) so that it is usual to find the two varieties of family name: Keefe and O'Keefe; Sullivan and O'Sullivan, Brien and O'Brien, and so on. With each invasion of Ireland there was an infusion of new names, to be eventually prefixed with Mac and O'; and with each mass emigration these names were exported widely – which is why you'll usually find an O'Grady or an O'Donnell in any telephone directory anywhere in the world.

Perry	(Also Perrie, Pirie) *Pirige*, Anglo-Saxon for pear, so the name probably derives from families growing pears or making perry
Pitman	*Pyttmann*, Anglo-Saxon term for a man living in a hollow

Potts	(Also Pott, Philpot) Originates from the family pet name of Philipot, or 'little Phillip'
Powell	Welsh, son of Howel or Howell
Power	*Pohier*, a citizen of Picardy; the name entered Ireland with the Anglo-Normans
Pratt	From the Old English *proett* = trick, and thus a nickname for a trickster
Price	Welsh, son of Rhys, a name dating from the fourteenth century
Prowse	*Prouz*, an old term for somebody courageous. As a name, a Richard le Prouz lived in Hertfordshire in the early thirteenth century
Putnam	Descendants of families that could have lived in either Puttenham, Surrey, or Puttenham, Herts
Quick	*Cwicu*, Anglo-Saxon for fast and alert
Quinn	*Conn*, Gaelic for an advisor
Ramsay	(Also Ramsey) A Scottish name but originates from Simund de Ramesie of Ramsey, England, to establish a new home in Scotland
Rank	From the Old English *rane* = strong and proud
Rawlinson	From the Teutonic forename Ralf
Read	(Also Reed, Reid) *Ried*, Anglo-Saxon for a clearing, appears to be the origin of these names, although an association with reeds could also provide a source
Rees	*Ris*, old Welsh for eager
Reeves	*Refa*, Anglo-Saxon for a judicial official. A Richard de Reves lived in Lancashire in the fourteenth century
Reid	See Read

Reilly	Irish, from an ancient Gaelic family name
Reynolds	From the Norman forename Reinald
Richardson	Son of Richard, one of the most common medieval first names. Many other surnames were spun off Richard, including Rix and even Higgins
Robertson	Son of Robert
Ross	Descendants of families that came to Kent from France before the eleventh century
Ryan	From the old Gaelic first name *Rian*
Ryman	A name linked with Rye and other marshy and coastal areas
Sainsbury	From Saintbury, Gloucestershire
Sampson	(Also Samson) Of considerable antiquity and possibly of Breton origin
Sargent	From the office of sergeant, highly ranked in medieval times
Saunders	Derives from Sander, a shortened version of Alexander used around the thirteenth century
Sawyer	A sawyer of wood in a sawpit
Sayer	A forename of Norman origin
Schaeffer	(Also Schafer, Schaffer) Derived from the Old German and Jewish name for a shepherd
Schneider	(Also Snider, Snyder) Derived from the Old German and Jewish name for a tailor
Schwartz	From the German-Jewish nickname for anyone dark and swarthy
Shaw	(Also Shea) In medieval times, a dweller in the wood. Other families could have taken their name from one or other of the places called Shaw
Sinclair	Scottish version of the Norman place-name *Saint Clair* and an old Caithness family name

Skeggs	From the Old Norman *skegg* = bearded one
Smart	*Smeortan*, Anglo-Saxon for pain; later to mean sharp and lively

---

The Smith family
The Smiths have proliferated since the first of their kind was known as a *smid*, or blacksmith, in Anglo-Saxon times. Now we not only have the ubiquitous Smith family, but Smithers, Smithson, Smyth, Smythe, Smit and a growing number of Smith-Greens, Smith-Camerons and a hundred other hyphenated combinations. Then there are the Arrowsmiths, Sixsmiths, Goldsmiths and, to come full circle, Blacksmiths. Take a bow, Ecceard Smid, Britain's very first Smith, who was alive a century before 1066.

Spark	From a medieval nickname meaning high-spirited
Stephenson	(Also Stimpson) Son of Stephen, a forename of Greek origin
Stewart	(Also Steward, Stuart) *Stigweard*, Anglo-Saxon for steward, a senior official of a manor
Sullivan	Derived from the old Gaelic personal name, *Suileabhain* = hawk-eye black
Sutherland	Descendant of someone from the former county of Sutherland
Talbot	*Talebot*, Breton for lampblack and a nickname for brigands; many fought for William the Conqueror in 1066 and stayed
Thompson	Son of Thomas, Thom or Tom

Thrower	Descendants of families in the silk trade
Tilley	*Tilia*, Anglo-Saxon for a farmer
Tinker	Inevitably associated with pots and pans and the mending of; a common surname in southern England
Tomkinson	Son of Tomkin, in turn a family nickname for 'Little Tom'
Tremaine	(Also Tremayne, Truman) From the Old Cornish *tre-men* = stone place
Trevor	From the Gaelic *Treabhair* = town-big, probably with some kind of industry
Tucker	Descendants of families of clothmakers
Turnbull	A Yorkshire name, deriving from a nickname meaning strong
Turner	*Tornour*, French for a craftsman with wood
Vaughan	*Fychan*, Old Welsh for small
Venables	Descendants of families from Venables, France, probably via Lancashire, where William de Venables lived during the thirteenth century
Vine	From a nickname for a vineyard worker
Wade	From *Wada*, a popular Anglo-Saxon name deriving from a fabled sea monster
Wagner	From the Teutonic for a wagon builder or driver
Wagstaff	A nickname for a beadle
Wainwright	*Waegnwyrhta*, Anglo-Saxon for wagon builder
Waite	Nickname for a nightwatchman
Walker	Descendants of clothworkers
Wall	Someone who lived near a wall (eg the Roman Wall, or a city wall)

Warren	Of French origin; a William de Warene is mentioned in the Domesday Book
Waterhouse	A family that lived near water
Watkins	Wat-kin, a family nickname for Walter
Weber	Descendants of weavers
Weston	For some reason, Weston was a common place-name and it gradually came into use as a surname; Godwinus de Westuna is recorded in the Domesday Book
Whatman	From the Anglo-Saxon description of bold and brave
Wheatcroft	Derives from the owner or tenant of a small enclosed field in which wheat is grown
Whitbread	A baker, but distinguished by a name that denoted he baked white, not common, bread
White	*Hwita*, Anglo-Saxon for fair-haired
Wilcox	(Also Wilcock) Derived from the very common forename William
Wild	(Also Wilde, Wilder) A fairly common prefix, indicating its owner was a bit on the wild side – hence Wildman and Wildsmith
Wilkinson	Son of Wilkin or Will
Williams	The common Norman forename of William was avidly used by the Welsh as a surname
Wilson	Son of Will or William
Wise	*Wis*, Anglo-Saxon for good judgement
Wren	(Also Wrenn) From the bird, small and clever
Wyman	Derives from the Anglo-Saxon first name Wigmund
Yapp	Ancient nickname for a cunning person

Last names

A gentleman named Hero Zzyzzx of Madison, Wisconsin, USA, is on record as being the ultimate last name in any telephone book anywhere. It's not a made-up name, either; he is the son of Xerxes Zzyzzx (pronounced Zizz-icks, by the way), and the name is a complex amalgam of Lithuanian, Finnish, German, Russian, French and other miscellaneous middle-European backgrounds.

If you've browsed through our list of the more common surnames in Britain, you will have noticed the following:

- The majority of names derive from the Anglo-Saxons, the later Scandinavian invaders, and from the Celts, who brought new names to south-west England, Wales, Ireland and Scotland.
- After the Normans there were no further invasions and most of today's family names were established during the four centuries after 1066, although the spellings of many of them have changed, some several times.
- Many of our surnames derive from first names (like Gilbert, Lucas or Daniel); from the father's name (Dennison, son of Denis); and nicknames (Fairfax, the fair-haired).
- A good many surnames can be linked to a trade, such as Falkner (originally a falconer); Milner (a flour miller); and self-evident derivations like Barber, Glover and Hooper.
- Place-names, particularly villages, manorial estates and farms often provided the inspiration for a family's name.

Finally, there are traps for the unwary. Although a surname like Sharp or Sharpe can be traced back to a nickname for someone who was quick and clever, and Strong or Strang to a person of great strength, other, similar names cannot be linked to characteristics they suggest. The forebears of a Mr Smellie had nothing to do with nightcarts or manure, and those of a Mr Swindle were probably not crooks: a smellie was someone who lived near a cultivated area or garden, and the Swindles came from Swindale, Westmorland.

Tracing Your Own Family Name

Ninety per cent of surnames can be traced fairly easily. Your first port of call should be your local library which should have several reference books on the subject. The most comprehensive and up-to-date of these is *A Dictionary of Surnames* by Patrick Hanks and Flavia Hodges (Oxford University Press, 1988), which gives the origins of around 70,000 names.

If you are unsuccessful, it is possible that your name may derive from a place-name – and probably one that is insignificant or even non-existent. To follow this line of enquiry you will need detailed county lists of place-names such as those of the English Place Name Society which, again, should be available through a library. Keeping in mind that the spelling may have changed over the centuries, you are almost certainly in for a long slog.

If you are still out of luck yet still determined, you will very likely need the help of a genealogist with access to specialist source material. Somewhere, some time, one of your ancestors bore your name for the first time. Good hunting!

Double-Barrelled Names

What happens when, as in *The Times*' Engagements column in the late 1970s, it is announced that John Anstruther-Gough-Calthorpe is to marry Lady Mary Gaye Cooper-Key? Mr John Anstruther-Gough-Calthorpe was, as it happened, the son of an old friend of Lady Mary's father, Lord Howe; but had he been a relative, the joint resulting surname could have been Cooper-Key-Anstruther-Gough-Calthorpe. And if you think this is going too far, it is still way short of what was until 1917 Britain's longest surname: Tollemache-Tollemache-de Orelana-Plantagenet-Tollemache-Tollemache – a true, copper-bottomed six-barrelled name. The last five-barrelled surname, which belonged to Lady Caroline Jemima Temple-Nugent-Chandos-Brydges-Grenville, disappeared when she died in 1946.

This business of hyphenated surnames seems to be peculiarly British, although there is on record a Lili Froelich-Bum, which distinctly lacks an all-British ring to it. While in Brazil, Pafia Pifia Pefia Pofia Pufia Da Costa lives serenely without a single hyphen in sight, in Britain we appear to need those little linking strokes to help us join the bits of names together, rather like a child's spell-ing prim-er. Why else would Mr Thomas Strangeways Pigg change his name to Mr Thomas Pigg-Strangeways?

The four-, three- and double-barrelled names, however, are disappearing fast. The Montagu-Stuart-Wortley-Mackenzies have dropped the Mackenzie; Lord Hovell-Thurlow-Cumming-Bruce is plain Lord Thurlow; and the Lyon-Dalberg-Actons now prefer to be known as the Actons. Fortunately for the hyphen, though, Britain's best-known triple-barrel, the explorer

Sir Ranulph Twisleton-Wykeham-Fiennes, intends to hang on to his birthright, at least for the time being.

The Names We Are Given

Surnames come with the family whether we like them or not, and there is not a lot we can do about our surnames except to go through the confusion and palaver of changing them.

The same may be said about first, given or Christian names; we have to settle for what our parents thought was right for us at the time. Unfortunately this delicate business of choosing names for offspring is often performed under complex circumstances ('I like Kimberley myself, but Fred prefers Hedwig which was his grandmother's middle name, and Mum wants Bryony – she's always wanted a kid with a Welsh name – so we're going to call her Sarah Diana'), not to mention such influences as fashion and alcohol. Still, whatever the names we were given by our parents, we in turn can exercise this naming power when we, in turn, become parents.

With over 5000 million individuals now on this earth and growing in numbers every day, we cannot be blamed for wondering if our individuality is a bit of a myth. There are 5000 million people with names, too; how many namesakes do we have out there? So we can hardly be blamed for trying to invent a bit of individuality for our children, and for attaching far more importance to names than perhaps they deserve.

Given names are of greater antiquity than surnames, many of which sprang from them. The first names came with the Romans, but the only ones to survive are Celtic corruptions changed out of all recognition. The earliest, surviving, identifiable names are those of the Germanic tribes, usually consisting of two descriptive words. *Berin-hard* is of Teutonic origin, meaning Bear-steadfast. The Anglo-Saxons changed it slightly, to *Beorn-heard*, a meaning Brave-steadfast. In time this became Barnard and then Bernard. Today we not only have Bernard, but the feminine Bernadette and the shortened form Bernie.

As with our surnames, Britain's stock of first names grew in size and variety with successive invasions: the Anglo-Saxons, the Scandinavians and the Normans. The Normans introduced Breton names and, more significantly, Latin names – mostly those of saints. So out went the Athelwulfs and Aethelwines, and in came the Richards and Williams – so that by the fourteenth century, two-thirds of England's male population were named Henry, John, William, Richard and Robert.

The spread of Christianity and the Old and New Testaments offered an entire hoard of Hebrew names to eager parents, as did the Renaissance with mellifluous classical Greek and Roman names like Minerva, Hypatia and Cassandra. And the Reformation and the Puritan ethic made their contribution, too, with Faith, Hope and Charity, not to mention Earth, Dust, Ashes, Tribulation and one If-Jesus-Christ-Had-Not-Died-For-Thee-Thou-Hadst-Been-Damned Barebones; he later changed it, sensibly enough, to Nicholas Barbon. These major endowments were followed by numerous other influences and fashions: floral names, gem names, pet names (Elizabeth alone spawned several dozen, including Lillibet, Bess, Betty, Eliza, Elspeth, Beth and Libby) and even recycled surnames, introduced with great flair by the Americans: Washington Irving being an early example. Even today new names are arriving with their owners from Africa and the Indian subcontinent, and Kashmira, Jameela, Ayesha and Azura are beginning to thread their way into Britain's already dense fabric of given names.

The following list of first names – girls first – is representative rather than complete; for more comprehensive collections, several readily-available books are suggested in the reading list at the back of this book.

So many first names are pet versions of a name (Meg

or Marge for Margaret), diminutives (Lucy for Lucinda), or alternative spellings (Kerry, Kerrie), that it is sometimes expedient to group the variations under the principal name (the *Guinness Book of Names* lists twenty-three variants of Jacqueline recorded on birth certificates!); however when a derivative has for a long period been a name in its own right it is shown separately.

As for the veracity of the meaning of names, those given here are generally accepted by genealogists and onomasticians (students of names) as not being too wide of the mark; at the same time it would be wise not to take them too literally.

Girls' Names

Abigail	Hebrew: 'father's joy'. Abbr. Abby, Gail, Gayle
Ada	German: 'happy'. Used in England from eighteenth century
Adelaide	Old German *adal*: 'nobility'; very popular after Queen Adelaide came to the throne in 1830
Adèle	French derivative of the German *adal* and Adela
Agatha	Greek: 'good'; popular in medieval period
Agnes	Greek: 'chaste, pure'; St Agnes ensured its wide popularity and there are many versions: Annis, Nessa and Netta; Agneta and Inez are foreign forms
Aileen	See Eileen
Alexandra	Greek: 'man's defender'; feminine of Alexander made popular in nineteenth

century by Princess Alexandra of
Denmark. Abbr. Alexis, Sandra,
Sandy, Zandra

Alice   Greek: 'truth' and to England as Alys
via France

Alison   A variation of Alice

Althea   Greek: 'wholesome', from seventeenth
century. Abbr. Thea

Amanda   Latin: 'worthy of love'. Abbr. Mandy

Amelia   Old German: 'labour'. Abbr. Emily

Amy   Old French: 'to love'. Popular in
nineteenth century

Andrea   Feminine of Andrew and fairly recent

Angela   Greek: 'messenger'. Feminine form of
angel

Anita   Hebrew: 'graceful'; the name re-
entered England as a Spanish variant
of Ann

Ann, Anne A truly international name derived
from the Hebrew: 'graceful'. And
Hannah: 'God has favoured me'. In
use for a thousand years in many
variants: Anna (England, Germany,
Holland); Anja, Anouska (Russia);
Anne, Annette (France); Anita
(Spain). Abbr. Nan, Nancy, Nana

Annabel   Norman: 'lovable'. Known in Scotland
from twelfth century

Arabella Almost certainly a variant of Annabel.
Abbr. Bel, Bella, Belle, Ella, Ellie

Arlene   Gaelic; possibly an abbreviation of
Charlene, feminine of Charles, or a
variation of Adeline. Abbr. Lena

Audrey   From the Anglo-Saxon Etheldreda,
meaning 'noble'

Augusta   (Also Augustina) Feminine of
Augustus, from the Latin: venerable.
Abbr. Gussie, Tina

Ava	Obscure, but possibly a corruption of Avis or Eva
Barbara	Greek: 'stranger'. Popularised by St Barbara, third century. Abbr. Babs, Barbra, Babette
Beatrice	(Also Beatrix) Latin: 'bringer of joy'. Popular through Shakespeare and Dante. Abbr. Bea, Trixie. The Welsh form is Bettrys
Becky	See Rebecca
Belinda	Old German: 'snake-like'. Abbr. Bel, Linda
Berenice	(Also Bernice) Greek: 'bringer of victory'
Bernadette	Feminine of Bernard from the Old German: 'resolute'. Popular with Roman Catholics because of St Bernadette of Lourdes
Bertha	Old German: 'bright'. First used as Berta in England. More common in France as Berthe
Beryl	Named after the precious stone of the same name
Bess	Pet form of Elizabeth
Beth	Shortened form of Elizabeth, made popular by one of the sisters in Louisa M. Alcott's *Little Women*
Betty	(Also Bettine, Bette, Betsy) Variant of Elizabeth
Beulah	Hebrew: 'matron'
Beverley	From Beverley, Yorkshire
Billie	Variation of Wilhelmina, German feminine of William
Blanche	French: *blanc* = white. In use from fourteenth century
Bobbie	From Roberta, feminine of Robert

Announcing Miss ABCDE Pepper

In December 1880 a Mr and Mrs Pepper found just enough room on the birth certificate for their daughter's name: Anna Bertha Cecilia Diana Emily Fanny Gertrude Hypatia Inez Jane Kate Louise Maud Nora Ophelia Quince (Quince??) Rebecca Starkey Teresa Ulysis (yes, Ulysis) Venus Winifred Xenophon Yetty Zeno Pepper.

Bonny	Scots: fair, pretty
Brenda	Old Norse: 'sword'. Introduced by the Vikings, it was in wide use in the Shetlands and popularised in the nineteenth century by Sir Walter Scott in *The Pirate*
Bridget	Celtic: 'mighty one'. Originally made popular by the sixth-century St Bridgit of Kildare who founded the first convents in Ireland. Abbr. Bridie, Biddie
Bronwen	Ancient Welsh: 'white bosom'
Bryony	Named after the hedgerow flower
Caitlin	Irish version of Catherine or Kathleen
Camilla	Etruscan. She was a Queen in Virgil's *Aeneid*
Carlotta	(Also Carla, Carly) Old German. Feminine forms of Charles, Carl and Karl
Carmel	Hebrew: 'garden'. From Mt Carmel in Israel and the Order of Carmelite nuns
Caroline	Feminine of Charles. Abbr. Carrie, Carolyn
Cassandra	Greek. A Trojan priestess whose fate was not to be taken seriously. Abbr. Cass, Sandie, Sandy

Catherine	(Also Catharine and Katherine) Greek: 'pure'. The name was in common use in Henry VIII's time; three of his wives were Catherines. There are many variations: Cathy, Catarine, Catriona, etc
Cecilia	Feminine of Cecil and popular since second-century St Cecilia, patron saint of music. Abbr. Cicely, Ciss
Celia	Latin: 'heavenly'
Charlene	Feminine form of Charles
Charlotte	Seventeenth-century feminine version of Charles
Charmaine	Variation of Carmel
Cheryl	Modern variation of Charlotte
Chloe	Greek: 'green shoot'. Variation Cloris
Christabel	Medieval name from the Latin made famous in Coleridge's 1816 poem, *Christabel*. Abbr. Chris
Christine	Anglo-Saxon: 'Christian'. One of a large family of names based on the word Christen
Cindy	Version of Cynthia or Lucinda
Clare	(Also Claire, the French version) Latin: 'bright'
Claudia	Feminine derivation from the Roman Claudius families
Clementine	Latin: 'merciful'. Feminine form of Clement
Clodagh	Irish, after the river in Tipperary
Colette	Shortened form of Nicole and Nicolette
Colleen	Old Irish: 'girl'
Constance	Latin: 'constancy'. Abbr. Connie
Cynthia	Greek: 'from Mt Cynthus'. Rarely used until in 1866 Mrs Gaskell used the name in her novel, *Wives and Daughters*

The Top Ten Girls' Names in England & Wales, USA and Australia

ENGLAND & WALES (1)	(2)	USA (3)	AUSTRALIA (4)
Rebecca	Emily	Ashley	Jessica
Sarah	Charlotte	Jessica	Sarah
Jessica	Olivia	Amanda	Emma
Hannah	Sophie	Sarah	Lauren
Lauren	Lucy	Brittany	Rebecca
Emma	Emma	Megan	Ashleigh
Sophie	Sarah	Jennifer	Amy
Samantha	Georgina	Nicole	Emily
Chloe	Alice	Stephanie	Kate
Catherine	Hannah	Katherine	Katherine

(1) *Mail On Sunday*, January 1992 from 2,100 births registered during random weeks at various registry offices throughout Britain in 1991. (2) *The Times* Top Ten for 1991 compiled from its announcement columns. (3) *Guinness Book of Names*, 1991. (4) Australian Registry Statistics, 1990.

Dana Feminine version of Daniel

Daphne Greek: 'laurel': one of Apollo's lovers who turned into a bush

Dawn Thought to be the creation of a romantic novelist

Debbie Short form of Deborah

Deirdre Probably Celtic; a popular Irish name

Delia (Also Cordelia) From the Greek island of Delos. Abbr. Dee, Didi

Denise Feminine of Denis; from the Greek Dionysius

Désirée French: 'desired'

Diana (Also Diane) Latin name for the Greek

	goddess of the moon and hunting. Abbr. Di, Dee
Dilys	Welsh: 'perfect'. In use from nineteenth century
Dinah	Hebrew: name of one of Jacob's daughters

How Dolores became Lolita

Of Spanish origin, Dolores was the name of the young heroine of Vladimir Nabokov's controversial 1955 novel, *Lolita*. As Nabokov's hero Humbert Humbert explains it: 'She was Lo, plain Lo, in the morning, standing four feet ten in one sock. She was Lola in slacks. She was Dolly at school. She was Dolores on the dotted line. But in my arms she was always Lolita.' And there you have it: Dolores/Dolly/Lola/Lo/Lolita.

Dora	Short form of Dorothy
Doreen	Irish derivative of Dorothy
Doris	Greek: a woman from the Dorian tribe
Dorothy	(Also Dorothea and Theodora) Greek: 'gift of God'. The origins of this name date back to St Dorothea of the third century, although it did not take hold in England until the sixteenth century. There are numerous variations: Doll, Dolly, Dora, Doreen, Dorinda, Dot, Dotty, Dory, Dodie and, in Dickens, Dorrit
Dulcie	Latin: 'sweet'; short form of Dulcibelle
Dymphna	Irish: 'worthy'
Edith	Anglo-Saxon: from Eadgyth, the tenth-century daughter of King Edgar. Abbr. Edie, Eydie

Edna	Hebrew: 'happy new life'. In use from nineteenth century
Edwina	Anglo-Saxon: feminine form of Edwin: 'rich friend'
Eileen	(Also Aileen) Greek: 'bright'
Elaine	Old French form of Helen
Eleanor	One of several medieval French forms of Helen. Variations include Eleanora, Elenore, Elinore, Ella, Ellie, Elly, Lenore, Leonora, Nell, Nellie, Nelly and Nora
Elen	(Also Ellen) Welsh form of Helen

Elizabeth

From the Hebrew *Elisheba* ('God is my satisfaction') via the Latin Elizabetha, we arrive at Elizabeth (Elisabeth in continental Europe) and multitudinous spin-offs: Liz, Lizzie, Liza, Eliza, Lillibet, Bess, Bessie, Betsy, Bette, Betty, Bettina, Elly, Elsa, Elsie, Elspeth, Elyse, Isobel, Lisette, Lise, Beth, Libby and a good many more.

Emily	From the Roman family name Aemeliis or Aemelius. As Emelye it was popularised by Chaucer
Emma	Old German: 'universal'; possibly a shortened version of Ermintrude. In use as Emma from eleventh century
Emmanuelle	Feminine version of the Hebrew name Emanuel
Enid	Celtic: 'soul'
Erica	Old Norse feminine form of Eric
Esme	Latin: 'loved'; a short form of Esmeralda
Estelle	French: 'star'

Esther	Possibly of Persian origin; one of the books in the Old Testament
Ethel	Anglo-Saxon: 'noble'; a name that has survived almost in its original form: Aethel
Eunice	Greek: 'great victory'; the Biblical mother of Timothy
Eve	From the Latin Eva but originally Hebrew
Evelyn	From the Norman Aveline, and originally a surname
Fanny	A variant of Frances
Fay	A nineteenth-century abbreviation of Faith
Felicity	Latin: 'happiness'
Fenella	Gaelic: 'white shoulders'
Fiona	A nineteenth-century creation from the Gaelic: 'fair'
Flora	Roman goddess of flowers
Florence	Latin: 'blooming'. As Florentius and then Florence it was also a masculine name. Abbr. Florrie, Flo, Floris, Flossie
Frances	(Also François in France; Francesca in Italy; Francisca in Spain) Latin: 'woman of France'. Variants include Fran, Fanny, Francine, Frankie, Franny
Gail	Shortened form of Abigail
Gaynor	From the Old Welsh Guinevere ('fair'), wife of King Arthur
Genevieve	An old French name: St Genevieve was the fifth-century patron saint of Paris
Georgina	Femine form of George
Geraldine	Feminine form of the Old German Gerald
Gertrude	Old German: 'strong spear'; Gertrude

48

	was one of the twelve Valkyries of old Norse mythology
Gillian	English version of Juliana, in turn the feminine form of Julian. Abbr. Gill, Julia, Julie
Gladys	An ancient Welsh name of uncertain origin
Glynis	Celtic: 'little valley'
Grace	Latin: *gratia* = 'grace'. Used as a name from thirteenth century
Greta	German and Scandinavian abbreviation of Margaret
Gwendolyn	Welsh: 'fair, blessed'. Abbr. Gwen, Wynne, Winnie
Hannah	Hebrew: 'God has favoured me'. Mother of Samuel the prophet. Abbr. Ann, Nancy
Hayley	An old English surname ('hayfield')
Hazel	From the German, named after the shrub

Floral names

Erica, Iris and Laurel are fairly common leftovers from the nineteenth-century craze for naming girls after plants and flowers. Perhaps the craze should be revived, as many plant-names are delightfully melodious: Acacia, Acantha, Amarylis, Artemisia, Daisy, Daphne, Jonquil, Hebe and Heather . . . for further inspiration, pick up any good gardening book!

Heidi	From Adalheid, the German version of Adelaide
Helen	Greek: 'bright'; popularised by fourth-century St Helena. Variants include

	Helena, Helene, Aileen, Eileen, Eleanor, Elena, Ellen, Elaine, Ilene, Lana, Lena
Hermione	Feminine of Hermes, the Greek messenger
Hilary	Latin: 'cheerful'
Hilda	Anglo-Saxon: 'war'
Hope	A Puritan name, often given to a triplet; the others were named Faith and Charity
Ida	Old German: 'labour'
Imogen	The heroine in Shakespeare's *Cymbeline*
Ingrid	From the name of an Old Norse god. Abbr. Inga
Irene	Greek: 'peace'; relatively recent in Britain
Isabel	(Also Isobel) Hebrew: 'God is my satisfaction'. A variant of Elizabeth, via Spain. Abbr. Ilsa, Belle, Ella, Ellie
Ivy	From the plant name, introduced in the nineteenth century
Jacqueline	From the French feminine of Jacques

Jane, Jean and Joan

These three names, and dozens of variants of them, all originate from John, through Johanna, Joanna and, by the sixteenth century, Joan, with Jane finishing strongly in the eighteenth century. Some of the variants include Jan, Janet ('Little Jane'), Janette, Janice, Janie, Jenny, Jeannie, Jeanette, Jeanne, Juanita and Jayne.

Jennifer	As Jenifer, the Old Cornish rendition of Guinevere
Jenny	(Also Jennie) 1920s short form of Jennifer
Jessica	Hebrew: 'God beholds'; also Shylock's daughter in Shakespeare's *The Merchant of Venice*
Jill	From Juliana, in turn from the Roman family name Julius
Joan	See Jane. Abbr. Jo, Joni, Jo-Ann
Joanna	See Jane
Jocelyn	An early Gothic (seventh-century) masculine name, but introduced only recently for girls
Jodie	Hebrew: 'Jewish woman'; a version of Judith
Josephine	Feminine form of Joseph, from the Hebrew. Abbr. Jo, Jolene, Josie, Jo-Jo and Fifi
Joy	Latin: 'Rejoicing'. Appeared in the twelfth century, disappeared, and rediscovered in the nineteenth century
Joyce	Celtic, probably from the seventh-century Breton St Jodoc; used until recently for both sexes
Judith	(Also Judy) Hebrew: 'Jewish woman'; feminine form of Judah
Julia	Feminine version of Julius, a Roman surname, which became popular in the eighteenth century from Shakespeare's *Two Gentlemen of Verona*. Variations include Julie, Jillian, Jill, Leanne and Leana
June	From the month of the same name
Justine	Latin: '*just*'; feminine form of Justin
Karen	Danish version of Katharine
Kate	Popular short form of Katharine
Katharine	(Also Katherine and Catherine) Greek:

'pure'. Exactly where, when and why the name parted with two different spellings is something of a mystery. The Latin 'K' spelling is the oldest. Variations include Kate, Katerina, Kathleen, Kathryn, Katie, Katrina, Kay, Kaye, Kit, Kittie, Kitty, Trina

Kathleen   (Also Cathleen) Irish version of Katharine

Kelly   From the Irish surname

Kerrie   From Kerry in Ireland

Kimberley   A popular transition either from the English surname or the South African diamond mine

Kirsty   Scottish version of the Scandinavian Kirsten

Kylie   Australian adaptation of Aboriginal for a boomerang

Laura   From Laurencia, feminine form of Laurence

Lavinia   Origin obscure, but it appears in Virgil's *Aeneid*

Leah   Hebrew: 'cow' or 'heifer'. Jacob's first wife

Lee   Adapted from the surname

Leila   Persian: 'night'

Lena   Short form of Helena

Lenore   Short form of Eleanor

Leonie   Feminine form of Leon

Lesley   Scottish. Made popular by Robert Burns' poem, *Bonnie Leslie*. The masculine version is Leslie

Lillian   An old variation of Elizabeth

Lily   Originally a shortened version of Elizabeth and Lillian, but reintroduced during the nineteenth-century vogue for floral names. Abbr. Lil, Lilli

Calamitous conjunctions

Why did Mrs Baggs of Leicester name her daughter Wyn? Were Mr and Mrs Christmas having a little joke when they christened their daughter Mary? And why did a Wolverhampton vicar have to explain to Mr and Mrs Stew that it might not be the best idea in the world to christen their baby daughter Iris? These combinations are as nothing, however, to an Alabama telephone company employee named Pearl Harbour, Asa Miner of Rhode Island, Golden Pancake of Ohio, Fortunate Tarte of Vermont, Honor Roll of Birmingham, Alabama, and a lady from Centerville, Louisiana, named Needa Climax. Barbara Shaver, though, only had herself to blame when she married Harold Barber to become Barbara Barber, *née* Shaver.

Linda	From the Old German Lindi, introduced in the nineteenth century
Lindsay	From the Scottish surname. Abbr. Lynsey, Lyn
Liza	(Also Lisa) Short form of Elizabeth
Lois	A Biblical name (from *Timothy*) in use from seventeenth century
Loretta	From Loreto, the Italian shrine
Lorna	Name of the heroine in R. D. Blackmore's 1869 novel, *Lorna Doone*
Lorraine	French: from Lorraine in France
Louise	French feminine of Louis (Louisa is the Latin version). Abbr. Lou, Lulu, Loise, Luise
Lucille	(Also Lucasta) Latin: 'light'
Lucinda	Latin: 'light'. Abbr. Cindy, Sindy
Lucy	From the popular martyred fourth-century St Lucia

Lydia	Greek: 'woman of Lydia' (part of Turkey)
Lyn	(Also Lynn, Lynne) Short version of either Linda or Lynette, a version of the Welsh Eluned. It is also an abbreviation of Rosalind
Mabel	From Amabel (Latin: 'lovable'). Abbr. Mab, Maybelle
Madeleine	A version of Magdalene (St Mary Magdalene washed Christ's feet with her tears). Abbr. Maude, Maud, Magda, Maddy and sometimes Madge
Maggie	Short version of Margaret
Marcia	From the Roman family name Marcius, and is the feminine of Marcus and Mark. Abbr. Marcy, Marsha

Margaret

This name with its large brood has been traced back to ancient Persia, and means 'pearl', although in France and England it once meant a daisy. It has been well used by saints and martyrs (St Margaret of Antioch is the patron saint of childbirth) and by royalty in England, Scotland and most European kingdoms. Variants are widespread: Marge, Maggie, Maggs, Margot, Margie, Meg, Megan, Maisie, Greta, Gretel, Marguerite, Margareta, Marghanita, Margit, Margita, Margrethe, Marina and Margeaux. It may be of interest to note that the fashion model and grand-daughter of the novelist, Margeaux Hemingway, tired of being reminded of her father's boast that she was 'conceived on a bottle of Chateau Margeaux', has changed her name to Margot.

Maria	Latin version of Mary; used from the eighteenth century
Marianne	French form of Marion
Marie	French form of Mary which found popularity in Scotland
Marilyn	American combination of Mary and Lyn
Marion	(Also Marian) Originally meaning 'Little Mary' it is also a combination of Mary and Ann
Marjorie	Old Scottish version of Margaret
Martha	(Also Marthe in France) Aramaic: 'noble lady'

Mary

From the Hebrew *Mrym*, but its meaning is obscure. The name, with its deeply religious connotations, and its dozens of variations, has penetrated into most countries of the world. It is Mairi in Scotland, Mair in Wales and Ireland, Maria in Italy and Spain, Maja in Germany, Manon, Marie, Marian and Marianne in France, Marja in Yugoslavia, Mascha in Russia, Mame in America, to name but a few. Other more distant cousins include Moira, Mitzi, May, Meryl, Mimi, Minnie and Molly.

Maud	(Also Maude) Old German: 'battle strength'. As Matilda it came to England with the Normans to become Mahault and then Maud. In 1855 Tennyson made it sensationally popular among the Victorians with his poem, *Maud*
Maureen	Irish version of 'Little Mary'
Maxine	Feminine form of Max and Maximilian

May	After the month, and also a version of Mary
Melanie	Greek: 'dark haired'
Merle	From a French surname
Meryl	Possibly a combination of Mary-Louise
Mildred	Anglo-Saxon: 'Meek but strong'. Abbr. Millie
Millicent	Old German: 'work strong'. Dates from the eighth century
Mirabella	(Also Mirabel) Latin: 'wonderful'
Miranda	Latin: 'admirable'; a Shakespeare invention?
Miriam	From the Hebrew *Myrm*, from which Mary also sprang
Moira	Scottish version of Mary
Mona	Despite the Mona Lisa, it derives from an Irish saint, arriving in England in the nineteenth century
Monica	From the fourth-century St Monica, mother of St Augustine
Muriel	Celtic: 'bright sea'. Long used in Ireland, its newer variants include Meriel, Merril and Meryl
Myfanwy	Welsh: 'my fine one'. Abbr. Myf
Myra	A poetic creation by Lord Brooke in the seventeenth century
Nadia	(Also Nadine) From the Russian *Nadazhda*: 'hope'
Nanette	A version of Ann
Naomi	Hebrew: 'delight'. Naomi was the Biblical mother-in-law of Ruth
Natalie	Latin: 'Christmas child'. Once given to girls born at Christmas. Christmas boys were named Noel
Nellie	Version of Helen or Eleanor. Abbr. Nell
Nicole	(Also Nicola) Feminine form of Nicholas

Nina	Russian version of Ann
Nora	(Also Noreen) Shortened Irish version of Honora
Norma	Feminine form of Norman; used from mid-nineteenth century
Olga	A Russian name, from the Old Norse Helga
Olive	Latin: 'olive branch'. Introduced to England in the Middle Ages. Abbr. Livia, Nola
Olivia	Italian version of Olive
Olwen	Old Welsh: 'white footprints', from a story in the *Mabinogion* in which white trefoils sprang up wherever the beauty Olwen trod
Oria	Irish: 'golden lady'
Pamela	Coined in Sir Philip Sidney's *Arcadia* of 1590. Abbr. Pam, Pammie, Pamella
Patience	A virtuous Puritan name, introduced in the seventeenth century
Patricia	Feminine of Patrick. Abbr. Pat, Pattie, Patsy, Patty, Patti, Tricia, Trish
Paula	Originally the German feminine of Paul
Pauline	Latin: 'small'; also the French feminine of Paul. Abbr. Paulette, Polly
Pearl	Latin: 'pearl'; one of the many 'gem' names
Peggy	Short form of Margaret
Penelope	Wife of Odysseus in Homer's *Odyssey*. Abbr. Penny, Poppy
Penny	See Penelope
Philippa	Feminine of Philip. Abbr. Pippa
Phoebe	Greek: 'the shining one'; Phoebe was also goddess of the moon in Greek mythology

Phyllis	Greek: 'leafy'
Primrose	A nineteenth-century flower name
Priscilla	A Roman surname; also a Biblical name (*Acts* 18:2). Abbr. Cilla, Prissy
Prudence	Latin: 'prudent'. A medieval name revived by the Puritans in the seventeenth century. Abbr. Prudy, Pru, Prue
Rachael	(Also Rachel) Hebrew: 'ewe'. Abbr. Rae, Raquel
Rebecca	(Also Rebekah) Hebrew. Abbr. Becky
Regina	(Also Regine) Latin: 'queen'. Abbr. Gina, Raine
Rene	(Also Renée) Greek: 'peace'. From Renata
Rhoda	Greek: 'Woman from Rhodes'
Rhonda	Welsh: From the Rhondda valley
Rita	Short version of Margarita
Roberta	(Also Robina) Feminine of Robert
Rosa	See Rose
Rosalie	See Rose

A *Rose* by other names smells even sweeter

Although we think of this name as immemorially associated with the flower, it in fact derives from a very ancient German word, *hros*, meaning horse. It was in time Latinised to *rosa* and given to the genus *Rosa* of the *Rosacea* family of shrubs, now popularly known as the rose. From this beautiful flower it was inevitably used as a female name, and from it spring many variants: Rosie, Rhoda, Rosalie, Rosalind, Rosamund, Rosanna, Roseanne, Rosetta, Rosemary, Rosaleen, Rosmunda, Ros, Roz, Ronnie, Rose Marie, Romy and many, many more.

Rosalind	See Rose
Rosamond	(Also Rosamund) See Rose
Rosanna	See Rose
Rowena	Possibly Anglo-Saxon via the Welsh Rhonwen
Roxanne	The Persian wife of Alexander the Great
Ruth	Hebrew. First known in England in the sixteenth century
Sabrina	After the Latin name for the River Severn
Sadie	See Sarah
Sally	See Sarah
Samantha	Probably the feminine of Samuel. Abbr. Sam, Sammy
Sandra	Short version of Alexandra
Sarah	Hebrew: 'princess'; the wife of Abraham in the Old Testament. There are many versions: Sara, Sadie, Sally, Zara, Zarah
Selina	From the French name Céline
Shakira	Arabic: 'be grateful'
Sharon	Hebrew: the Biblical name for Palestine
Sheila	From the Irish form of Celia or Cecilia
Shelagh	Gaelic form of Cecily. Abbr. Sheela, Shelly
Shelly	(Also Shelley) Of mixed origin: from surnames like Shelley and Kelly; but also a short form of Rachel, Michelle, Sheila and Shelagh
Shirley	From an English place-name, it was popularised by Charlotte Brontë in her 1849 novel, *Shirley*
Sian	Celtic version of the ancient names Jane and Joan
Sibyl	(Also Cybil) Greek: 'woman of the oracle'

Felicitous names

Over the past several decades it has to be said that the top fifty girls' names lack a certain impetuousness, élan and, well, smouldering danger. Where are the Cassandras, the Perditas, the Delilahs? Or the head-turning Cosimas, Consuelas, Dominiques and Désirées? On the other hand, would your daughter thank you for naming her Divina, Godiva, Felicia or Ambrosine? Yet there still remains a wide and disarmingly mellifluous choice in the voluptuousness of girls' names, like these: Alethea, Aurelia, Clea, Delia, Dymphna, Flavia, Hypatia, Iseult, Sidony, Minerva, Mercedes, Ariana, Ariadne, Adriana, Calandra and Calypso.

Sylvia	(Also Silvia) Latin: 'wood' or 'forest'; the name of the mother of Romulus and Remus, and the subject of the famous Shakespeare line, 'Who is Sylvia, what is she?'. Abbr. Sylvie
Simone	Hebrew and the feminine of Simon, a New Testament name
Sinead	Feminine of Sean, Irish version of Jane or John
Siobhan	Irish version of Jane or John
Sonia	Russian form of Sophia
Sophia	(Also Sophie) Greek: 'wisdom'
Stacy	(Also Stacey) Shortened form of Anastasia, and possibly also Eustace
Stella	Latin: 'star'. In use from sixteenth century
Stephanie	Feminine of Stephen. Abbr. Stefanie, Steffie

Susannah	(Also Susan) Hebrew: 'lily'; Dates from the Old Testament account of Susannah and the Elders. Abbr. Susan, Sue, Suzanne, Suzy, Susie, etc
Tabitha	Aramaic: 'gazelle'. Abbr. Tabby
Tamara	Hebrew: 'data palm'. Abbr. Tammy
Tamsin	Aramaic: 'twin'. Derives from the feminine form of Thomas
Tanya	(also Tania) From the Russian form of Tatiana
Tara	From the ancient sacred hill in County Meath, Ireland and immensely popular after the name of the homestead in the novel *Gone With The Wind*
Teresa	Probably Spanish; popularised by the sixteenth-century St Theresa of Avila. Abbr. Tess, Tessa, Terri

Fashions in France

There is always a lot of name trading across the Channel and England has always borrowed heavily from France. But lately the French have been stealing such Anglo-Saxon names as Marion and Kevin. Over the last forty years, however, the most popular names for girls have remained steadfastly Gallic: Emilie, Aurélie, Céline, Stephanie, Sandrine, Nathalie, Brigitte, Martine and Françoise – but not necessarily in that order.

Theodora	(Also Theophilia) Greek: 'God's gift' or 'loved by God'. The name has inspired many spin-offs, including Thea, Dora and Tiffany

Theresa	See Teresa
Thora	Old Norse: 'thunder' from Thor, god of war
Tilly	A variation of Matilda
Tina	Short for names ending with 'tina, like Christina
Toni	Shortened version of Antonia
Tracy	(Also Tracey) Short version of Teresa
Tricia	Short version of Patricia
Trudy	Short version of Gertrude. Also Trudi, Trudie
Una	(Also Oona, Oonagh) Old Irish: 'lamb'
Unity	One of the seventeenth-century virtuous Puritan Christian names
Ursula	Latin: 'she-bear'. Popularised by the fifth-century martyred Briton St Ursula of Cologne
Valerie	From *Valerius*, a Roman family name. Abbr. Val
Valmai	Welsh: 'May blossom'
Vanessa	Coined by Jonathan Swift of *Gulliver's Travels* fame. Abbr. Nessa
Vera	Russian: 'faith'. Also short for Veronica
Verity	Latin: 'truth'. In use from the seventeenth century
Veronica	Latin: 'true image', possibly referring to the image of Christ's face, which she wiped as he carried his cross to the crucifixion; his image was supposed to have remained on the cloth of her veil
Victoria	Latin: 'victory'. Popular during and after the reign of Queen Victoria. Abbr. Vicki, Vickie, Victorine, Vita
Violet	A popular nineteenth-century flower name. Abbr. Vi, Yolande

Virginia	From the Roman family name Verginius. Abbr. Ginny, Ginnie, Ginger
Wanda	Teutonic: 'branch' (of a family). Popular after the heroine of nineteenth-century novelist Ouida's *Wanda*
Wendy	A character in J. M. Barrie's *Peter Pan* (1906).
Wilhelmina	German feminine of Wilhelm and made popular by the Hanoverian Royal Family. Abbr. Willa, Mina, Minna, Minnie, Wilma, Willa, Valma, Velma, Billie
Winifred	Old Welsh: Wenefreda, the Latin name for St Gwenfrewi, anglicised to Winifred in the eighteenth century. Abbr. Freda, Winnie
Yasmin	(Also Jasmine) Persian: 'jasmine flower'. Abbr. Jess, Jessame
Yvette	Feminine version of Yves. Abbr. Evette
Yvonne	Feminine version of Yves
Zara	Arabic: 'bright dawn'. Also an abbreviation of Alexandra
Zelda	Probably a shortened version of Griselda
Zoë	Greek: 'life'; originally a translation of the Hebrew for the Biblical Eve

Boys' Names

Aaron	Hebrew or Egyptian. The brother of Moses

Abraham	Hebrew: 'father of a multitude'. Abbr. Abe, Bram
Adam	Hebrew: 'red'; the Biblical first man
Adrian	Latin: 'Man of the Adriatic'
Alan	Of Celtic origin, coming to England with the Normans as Alain and Aleyn
Alastair	Scottish version of Alexander
Albert	Old German: 'noble and bright'. From Adalbert and Athelbert. Abbr. Al, Bert, Bertie
Alexander	Greek: 'defender'. A very early Christian name with many variants: Alex, Alec, Alick, Sandy, Alister, Alistair, Alastair
Alfred	An old Anglo-Saxon name, developing through Ealdfrith and Alfrid to the name borne by King Alfred the Great (AD 849–901). Abbr. Al, Alf, Alfie, Fred, Freddie, Freddy
Andrew	Greek: 'manly'. The first disciple called by Jesus and an immensely popular name through the hundreds of churches named after him. Abbr. Andy, Drew
Angus	Gaelic: 'one choice'. Popular in Scotland. Abbr. Gus
Antony	(Also Anthony) From the Roman family name Antonius. The name was forever popular after the exploits – as both soldier and lover of Cleopatra – of Mark Antony. Abbr. Tony, Anton
Archibald	Old German: 'bold'. Abbr. Archie
Arnold	Teutonic: 'eagle power'. Imported by the Normans
Arthur	Of Latin or Celtic origin, the name is historically linked with King Arthur and his Knights of the Round Table of medieval times. Abbr. Art, Artie
Ashley	Anglo-Saxon: 'ash wood dweller'

The middle name

For several generations it has been the practice to provide a child with a second, or middle, given name. This is handy when, in later life, the owner decides for some reason he or she doesn't care for the first choice. That is why Henry Beatty is rather better known as the actor Warren Beatty. Others known by their middle names include the broadcaster Alfred Alistair Cook, the Australian writer Vivian Clive James, the West Indian cricketer Isaac Vivian Richards, the novelist Ralph Hammond Innes and the former British Prime Minister, Leonard James Callaghan.

Aubrey	(Also Auberon) From the German Alberich via the French Auberi. Abbr. Bron
Augustus	Latin: 'venerable'. A title given to Roman emperors and other royalty. Abbr. Gus, August, Augie, Austin
Austin	See Augustus
Barnaby	English version of Barnabas, St Paul's travelling companion. Abbr. Barney
Barry	Celtic: 'spear'. Imported into England from Ireland in the nineteenth century
Bartholomew	Hebrew: 'son of a farmer'. Popular in England from the twelfth century. Abbr. Bartlemy, Bart
Basil	Greek: 'kingly'. The fourth-century St Basil the Great was an early holder of the name
Benedict	Latin: 'blessed'. Abbr. Ben, Benny
Benjamin	Hebrew: 'son of the right hand'; also Jacob's youngest son. It became very popular after the Reformation in the

	sixteenth century. Abbr. Ben, Benny, Benji
Bernard	Old German: 'brave as a bear'. Introduced by the Normans. Abbr. Bernie, Barney
Bert	Short version of names such as Albert, Herbert and Bertram
Bertram	Old German: 'bright raven'. Abbr. Bert, Bertie
Bevis	Introduced by the Normans as Beuves, then Beves
Bharat	Sanskrit: 'he who sustains'. Was brother of Rama
Bill	See William
Blake	From the medieval surname meaning 'dark'
Bob	See Robert
Brad	(Also Brady) Short version of Bradley, from the Anglo-Saxon: 'wood clearing'
Brendan	Name of a sixth-century Irish saint
Brett	(Also Bret) Of Breton or old English origin
Brian	(Also Brien, Bryan, Brion and Briant) Of Celtic origin, it became popular in Ireland from the eleventh century through the hero King Brian Boroimhe. It was, as O'Brien, also a widespread surname
Broderick	Old Welsh: 'son of Roderick'. Abbr. Brod
Bruce	Of Norman origin, it was popularised in the fourteenth century by King Robert the Bruce of Scotland
Carl	(Also Karl) German version of Charles
Cecil	From the Roman family name, Caecillius. Hardly known as a boy's name until the eighteenth century

Nicked names

What's missing from _ _ _ _ H E W to make it a well-known boy's name? Easy: Matt, to make it Matthew. Now try your hand at these (Answers on next page):

1 C H R I S _ _ _ _ _ _
2 _ _ _ _ L A S
3 C A M E _ _ _
4 _ _ _ _ A N D E R
5 _ _ Y S
6 _ _ _ _ A M I N
7 _ _ _ H U R
8 G R E G _ _ _
9 _ _ A A _
10 _ A N N _ _ _ L

Charles	Old German: *carl* = 'a man', which was latinized to Carolus and thence into French as Charles. It took off as a highly popular name through the exploits of Charlemagne, or Charles the Great and, later in England, by Kings Charles I and II. From this name spring many variants: Charlie, Charley, Carl, Karl, Carlo, Caryl, Carroll, Karel and, of course, Chuck and Chick
Chris	See Christopher
Christopher	Greek: 'bearer of Christ'. A very early Christian name which spread widely through the influence of St Christopher, patron saint of travellers and who was also supposed to protect against accidents and sudden death. Abbr. Chris, Kit, Kester
Clarence	Latin: 'famous'. Often used by royal families since the fourteenth century. Abbr. Clarrie
Clark	(Also Clarke) From the surname, meaning a cleric

67

Claude	(Also Claud) From the Roman family name Claudius
Clement	Latin: 'merciful'. Abbr. Clem

Answers to nicked names
1. ChrisTOPHER 2. DOUGlas 3. CameRON
4. ALEXander 5. RHys 6. BENJamin
7. ARThur 8. GregORY 9. ISaaC
10. HannIBAL

Clifford	From the old English place-name and surname and used as a first name since the nineteenth century. Abbr. Cliff
Clive	An old English surname which became a first name in honour of Anglo-Indian hero Sir Robert Clive
Colin	A name of mixed parentage, first as Col, a short form of the French Nicholas; then in medieval times as a nickname; and finally as a Gaelic term for a cub or pup and then as a nickname for a young man or a 'gay blade'
Connor	(Also Conor and Conan) From the Old Irish word *con* = high. Also, as O'Connor, a common surname
Conrad	Old German: 'bold counsel'. Abbr. Con, Connie, Curt, Kurt
Craig	Scottish: 'cliff' or 'crag'
Cyril	Greek: 'lord'. The ninth-century St Cyril introduced Christianity to the Slavic nations

The Top Ten Boys' Names in England & Wales, USA and Australia

ENGLAND & WALES (1)	(2)	USA (3)	AUSTRALIA (4)
Daniel	James	Michael	Matthew
Thomas	Alexander	Christopher	Daniel
Samuel	Thomas	Matthew	Michael
James	William	Joshua	Thomas
Christopher	Edward	Andrew	Benjamin
Jamie	Charles	Daniel	James
Adam	Oliver	Justin	Samuel
Michael	George	David	Nicholas
Alexander	Henry	Ryan	Joshua
Jack	Samuel	John	Christopher

(1) The *Mail on Sunday*, 1992, compiled from 2,100 births registered during random weeks at UK registry offices in 1991. (2) *The Times* Top Ten compiled from its announcement columns during 1991. (3) *Guinness Book of Records*, 1991 (non-white names were virtually identical but in a different order, and the one new name was Brandon). (4) Australian Registry Statistics, 1990.

Dai	Shortened Welsh version of David
Damian	Greek: 'to tame'. An early Christian martyr who died in Syria
Daniel	Hebrew: 'God has judged'. Although a popular name since Biblical times, hardly used in Britain until the Middle Ages. Abbr. Dan, Danny, Dannie
Darcy	From the Norman surname D'Arcy via a soldier who accompanied William the Conqueror
Darren	A twentieth-century invention of mysterious origin

Daryl Most likely Norman, after the placename Airel as in '*de Airel*'. Also spelled Darryl

David Hebrew: 'beloved friend'. A key character in the Bible, so it is not surprising that David has been a widely used name, although unknown in England until the Conquest. Because of the sixth-century Archbishop Dewi, the patron saint of Wales, David has always been popular with the Welsh. Variants include the Welsh Dai, Deio, Dafydd and Dewey, plus Dave and Davy

Dean From an Old English surname meaning 'valley dweller'

Denis (Also Denys and Dennis) Derives from the Greek name Dionysos. Abbr. Den, Dion

Derek (Also Deryk, Derrick) From the Old German name Theodoric and influenced by the Dutch version, Dirk

Desmond Gaelic: From the surname of families from South Munster in Ireland. Abbr. Des, Desi

Dick Short form of Richard

Dirk See Derek

Dominic Latin: 'of the Lord'. The twelfth-century St Dominic gave the name a boost in the Middle Ages. Abbr. Dom, Nick

Donald Celtic: 'ruler'. Surfaced first in the Scottish Highlands but also popular in Ireland, especially as Donal. Abbr. Don

Dougal (Also Dugald) From the Old Irish *dubhgall*, meaning 'dark stranger', which they called the Vikings

Douglas Celtic: 'dark blue'; originally a place

	or clan name in Scotland. Abbr. Doug, Duggie
Dudley	Anglo-Saxon: 'Dudda's (a Saxon) Wood', which became Dudley in Worcestershire, then a surname and finally a first name. Abbr. Dud
Duncan	Gaelic: 'brown warrior'
Dwayne	(Also Duane) From an Old Irish surname
Dylan	Old Welsh: 'son of the sea'
Eamonn	(Also Eamon) See Edmond
Edgar	Old English: 'happy spear'. Abbr. Ed, Eddy, Ned
Edmond	(Also Edmund) Old English: 'rich protector'. A royal Wessex, pre-Norman name and also that of the ninth-century St Edmund. Abbr. Eamonn (Irish); Ed, Eddie, Ned

---

Edward

This quintessentially English name derives from the Old English *Eadweard*, meaning 'rich or happy guardian'. It was the name of the two Wessex kings, Edward the Martyr and Edward the Confessor, the last Anglo-Saxon king who also founded Westminster Abbey. Because of these noble associations the name has remained popular throughout the millennium, also spreading across Europe as Edouard (France); Eduardo (Spain and Italy); Duarte (Portugal) and Edvard (Scandinavia).

| **Edwin** | Old English: 'happy friend'. The name of a seventh-century Christian king of Northumbria |

Elliot	(Also Elliott, Eliot) Derives from the less well-known Hebrew names Elijah and Elias, meaning 'Jehovah is God'. Abbr. Eli, Ellis
Elvis	Old Norse: 'all wise'. Known only as a surname until the advent of the singer Elvis Presley
Emlyn	Welsh version of the Roman family name Aemilius, its European equivalents being Emil and Emile
Eric	Teutonic: 'ruler'. Brought to England by the Viking invaders, unpopular after the Normans but revived in the nineteenth century. Abbr. Erik, Rick, Ricky
Ernest	Old German: 'earnest'. Introduced from Germany in the eighteenth century. Abbr. Ern, Ernie
Euan	(Also Owen and Ewan) Welsh version of John.
Eugene	Greek: 'well born'; the name of four Catholic Popes. Abbr. Gene
Evan	English version of Euan
Evelyn	Of Celtic origin, from the old surname Evelyn
Ewan	See Euan
Ferdinand	Old German: 'adventurer'. First found its way to Spain where its close association with the Catholic faith made it unpopular in England
Fergus	Celtic: 'chosen man'. Abbr. Fergie
Floyd	Modern version of the Welsh name Lloyd
Francis	Old German: 'one of the Frank tribe' or 'a man of France', which Gaul, overrun by the Teutonic Franks, eventually became. Its great and lasting popularity owed much to the

thirteenth-century St Francis of Assisi, and also to the similar Latin word *francus*, which meant free. Primarily a European first name (Franciscus, Francisco, Francresco, François and Franz), it was not so popular in Protestant England until the nineteenth century. Abbr. Frank, Frankie

Frank Short form of Francis

Frederick and Fred

From the Old German: 'peace ruler'. Until the eighteenth century it remained pretty much a Germanic name; then the Hanovers not only introduced it to Britain but popularised it to the point of overkill. As a result it is little used today, especially as it somehow acquired a belt-and-braces image; to be called a 'fred' is to be called gormless. To offset this image the Fred Society was created in the US in 1983 and numbers several thousand members, all named Fred or Freda. The Society's newsletter is called *The Fred Connection*.

Gareth Origin unclear but probably Welsh; it first appeared in the fifteenth-century tales of King Arthur. Abbr. Gary, Garry, Garth

Gavin From the German Gawin, through the Welsh Gawain. Gavin is thought to be the Scottish version

Geoffrey Old German: 'peace'. Seems to have evolved from the German Gaufrid, the Old French Geoffroi and medieval Geffrey. Abbr. Geoff, Jeff, Jeffrey

George	Greek: 'farmer'. In use since the third century St George, patron saint of England and Greece. Its popularity peaked in the eighteenth and nineteenth centuries
Geraint	From the Latin *Gerontius* from the Greek word meaning 'old'. It occurs in the Welsh *Mabinogion*
Gerald	Teutonic: 'spear rule'. Introduced by the Normans. Abbr. Gerry, Jerry, Gary, Gerallt (Welsh)
Gerard	See Gerald
Gilbert	Old German: 'bright pledge; introduced by the Normans. Abbr. Gill, Gib, Bert, Bertie
Giles	Greek: 'goat'. Reached England as Gilles in twelfth century
Glenn	(Also Glen, Glyn and Glynn) Celtic: 'valley'
Glyn	See Glenn
Godfrey	From the Old German Godafrid = 'God's peace'
Gordon	From the Old Scottish clan and family name
Goronwy	Old Welsh: 'hero'
Graham	(Also Grahame, Graeme) Originally from the place-name Grantham, called Graham in the Middle Ages, it was taken to Scotland as a clan name and surname
Grant	Old French nickname meaning 'tall man'
Gregory	(Also Gregor) Greek: 'watchful'. In use during Norman times but because of its Catholic associations it became unpopular until recently. Abbr. Greg, Gregg
Guy	Old German: 'wide' or 'wood'
Gwilym	Welsh version of William

MrWolfe590Sr.

Mr Wolfe 590 should have met Miss ABCDE Pepper (see Girl's names), for, with her, he shares the record for the world's longest name. Born in 1904, his name came to the world's attention in the 1960s for the simple reason that he was baptised Adolph Blaine Charles David Earl Frederick Gerald Hubert Irvin John Kenneth Lloyd Martin Nero Oliver Paul Quincy Randolph Sherman Thomas Uncas Victor William Xerxes Yancy Zeus Wolfeschlegelsteinhausenberger-dorff, Sr. – in all, 26 given names and a surname totalling 590 letters.

Hamish	From the Gaelic version of James
Harold	From the Old English Hereweald meaning 'army power' (although it did King Harold no good at Hastings), the modern name probably derives from the Norse Harald. Abbr. Harry, Hal, Errol
Harvey	Breton: 'battle worthy'
Henry	Old German: 'home ruler'. The French used the latinized Henri, which after the Normans became Henry. Widespread throughout Europe as Hendrik, Enrico, Enrique, Heinrich, Heinz, Arrigo and Henne. Abbr. Hal, Harry, Hank
Herbert	Teutonic: 'army bright'. Abbr. Herb, Herbie, Bert
Hilary	From the Latin *hilaris*, meaning 'cheerful', it became Hilarius and thence from the thirteenth century as a surname
Hiram	Hebrew: 'God is my brother'

Horace	(Also Horatio) From the Roman family name Horatius
Howard	Possibly from hayward, a medieval manor-minder, it was for centuries a noble surname
Hubert	Teutonic: 'bright spirit'. Abbr. Bert, Bertie
Hugh	(Also Hugo) Old German: 'mind' or 'heart', latinized to Hugo, and changed by the Celts to Huw. Abbr. Hew, Huey
Hugo	See Hugh
Humphrey	From the Old German Hunfrith, meaning 'peace giant'. A common medieval name (Humpty Dumpty was originally Humphrey Dumphrey).
Huw	See Hugh
Hywel	(Also Howel) Welsh: 'eminent'. Abbr. Hy
Ian	(Also Iain) Scottish version of John
Ifor	See Ivor
Irving	Originally an English place-name, then a Scottish surname
Irwin	(Also Erwin) Probably of Anglo-Saxon origin
Isaac	Hebrew: 'happy God'. Isaac was the Biblical son of Abraham and Sarah. Abbr. Ike (from Isaak), Zac
Ivan	Russian version of John
Ivor	(Also Ifor, Ivo) Origin obscure; possibly from the Old German: 'yew' via the French Yves, or from the Old Welsh: 'lord'
Jack	Short version of John
Jacob	Hebrew: 'supplanted'. Abbr. Jake
James	Oddly enough, the name we associate so closely with England's history did

not appear in this country until the twelfth century. It derives from the Hebrew Jacomus, the same in meaning and similar to Jacobus, which became Jacob. Jacomus became Jaime in Spain and one theory is that pilgrims brought it back from there. In one form or another it is globally popular. Abbr. Jim, Jimmie, Jamie, Jem

Jason   Greek version of the Hebrew name Joshua

Jeffrey   (Also Jeff) See Geoffrey

Jeremy   From Jeremiah, which in Hebrew means 'May God exalt'. Abbr. Jerry, Jem

---

Anagram that name, or name that anagram!

Wordsmiths find it fairly easy to form apposite anagrams of full names, like Florence Nightingale/Flit on, cheering angel, or Oliver Wendell Holmes/He'll do in mellow verse. Rather more demanding is the art of forming anagrams from a single first name, like Cathy/yacht, or Annie/inane. See if you can identify the names from the anagrams below. Answers on next page.

1 lace	5 warden	9 nailed	13 meagre
2 dolly	6 clean	10 wined	14 evils
3 anvil	7 larches	11 slime	15 ashen
4 yonder	8 regard	12 events	16 lyric

Jevon   Welsh version of John

Jim   Short form of James

Jocelyn   Old German: 'of the Goth tribe'. First a surname, then a masculine first name, now almost exclusively a girl's name. Abbr. Joss

Joe	Short form of Joseph
Joel	Hebrew: 'Jehovah is God'. A Norman name
John	From the Hebrew Johanen: 'Jehovah has favoured'. The name had a great start from the hundred or so saints named John, and from the Middle Ages it has remained the most ubiquitous of Christian names with a large international family of variants: Jon, Johnnie, Johnny, Jock, Evan, Euan, Ewan, Iain, Ian, Jan, Jean, Jens, Jevon, Johann, Johannes, Hans, Juan, Sean, Shuan, Sion, Owen and, of course, Jack
Jonathan	Surprisingly, the origin of this name is not the same as that of John. It derives from the Hebrew 'God has given'. Abbr. Jon
Joseph	Hebrew: 'May Jehovah greaten'. An Old Testament favourite of the Puritans. Abbr. Joe, Jo, Joey
Joshua	Hebrew: 'God is my salvation'. Another Biblical name used widely by the Puritans. Abbr. Josh, Jason
Julian	From the Roman family name Julius. Abbr. Jules
Justin	Latin: 'just'. The name of a second-century Christian martyr

---

Name that anagram
Answers

1 Alec	5 Andrew	9 Daniel	13 Graeme
2 Lloyd	6 Lance	10 Edwin	14 Elvis
3 Alvin	7 Charles	11 Miles	15 Shane
4 Rodney	8 Gerald	12 Steven	16 Cyril

Keith	Gaelic: 'wood'. Nineteenth-century adaptation from the Scottish surname
Kelvin	From the Scottish river and place-name. Abbr. Kel
Kenneth	From the Gaelic Cinaed or Cinead, and the name of the ninth-century first king of Scotland. Abbr. Ken, Kenny
Kevin	Old Irish: 'handsome birth'; popularised from the seventh-century St Kevin. Abbr. Kev
Kieran	Old Irish: 'dark haired'. A deeply rooted Irish name dating from the twelfth century
Kim	Short for Kimball O'Hara, the boy character in Rudyard Kipling's 1901 novel, *Kim*
Kit	Short form of Christopher
Lachlan	From the Gaelic name for the Vikings
Lancelot	Old German: 'land'. Popularised by Sir Lancelot, the hero of Arthurian legend. Abbr. Lance
Larry	Shortened form of Laurence
Laurence	(Also Lawrence) From the Roman city of Laurentium. Abbr. Laurie, Larry, Lawrie
Lee	Alternatives to Leo and Levi
Leo	Latin: 'lion'. Now eclipsed by other 'leo' names like Lee, Leon and Leonard
Leon	From the French Léon; popular in Jewish communities
Leonard	From the Old German Leonhard = 'lion bold'. In use from the Middle Ages and now has a range of variants: Len, Lenny, Leo, Leon, Lionel, Leander
Leroy	French: 'the king'. Mostly confined to the US

Leslie	From the Scottish surname after a place-name, from around the nineteenth century. Abbr. Les, Lee
Lester	From the place-name Leicester
Lewis	(Also Lew) See Louis
Liam	Irish version of William
Lionel	See Leonard. Means 'little lion'
Llewelyn	Old Welsh: 'lion leader'. It appears as Leolin in the thirteenth century. Abbr. Lew, Lewis, Lyn
Lloyd	From the Welsh *llwyd* = grey; also a common surname
Louis	(Also Lewis) Derives from the Old German meaning 'great battle', through the French Clovis to Louis, and ultimately through Lowis to Lewis, the English version, which arrived after the Normans. Abbr. Lou, Louie, Lew
Lucien	(Also Lucian) Latin: 'light'. An alternative to Lucius via the Latin name Lucianus
Ludovic	From Ludovicus, a Latin version of Lewis

Some mothers do have 'em (but why do they give 'em such crazy names?)

Neil Down, Luke Sharp, John Thomas O'Toole: all real names of real people. So are Ure A Pig, T Fud Pucker Tucker, Safety First (a doctor, incidentally), Peter Beter, Ivor Odor and Henry Will Burst. Crazy, yes, but presumably their parents must have known what they were doing. In the cases of William Charles Flush and Peter Enis, however, perhaps their parents did make honest, though unfortunate, mistakes.

Luke	(Also Lucas) Name of one of the Evangelists and in use in England from around the twelfth century
Malcolm	From the Gaelic *maol-Columb*, meaning disciple of the sixth-century St Columba, who founded Celtic Christianity and the monastery on Iona. Abbr. Mal
Manny	Short form of Emanuel
Mark	Originally from the god Mars, through the Latin Marcus
Martin	Like Mark, Martin derives from Martinus, which pertains to Mars. Popular from around the twelfth century. Abbr. Marty, Martie, Mart, Marten
Matthew	Hebrew: 'gift of God'. The name of the first Evangelist was introduced to England by the Normans. Abbr. Mat, Matt
Maurice	From the Latin Mauritius, meaning a person from Morocco – a Moor, and used as a first name from around the third century. Abbr. Maury, Morris
Maxwell	Maximilian used to supply the shortened version Max; now it derives almost exclusively from Maxwell, which itself springs from the Scottish surname
Melvin	(Also Melvyn) From a Norman surname which became Melville, a Scottish surname. Abbr. Mel
Mervyn	(Also Merlyn) Spun out of a group of Welsh surnames: Myrddin, Merfin, Mervin and used as a first name from the nineteenth century. Abbr. Merv, Marvin

Michael	Hebrew: 'who is close to the Lord'. Name of one of the Biblical archangels and of many saints. Abbr. Mike, Mick, Micky, Mickey, Mitch
Miles	(Also Myles) Origin obscure, but possibly from the Latin word for soldier. A Norman import
Morris	See Maurice
Murray	From the Scottish place-name Moray
Nat	Short version of Nathan and Nathaniel, both from the Hebrew: 'God's gift'
Ned	Short form of Edward, Edwin, Edgar and Edmund
Neil	(Also Neal, Neale and Nigel) According to some name experts, this name made a long round trip from Ireland (Niul) to Iceland and Scandinavia (Njal), then to Norman France (Nele) to be Latinized as Nigellus ('black') and finally back to Ireland as Niall. Neil now seems to be the most popular
Nelson	Means 'Neil's son'
Neville	Derived from Neuville in Normandy. Abbr. Nev
Nicholas	Greek: 'victory for the people'. Popularised, especially in Eastern Europe, by the fourth-century St Nicholas. Abbr. Nicolas, Nick, Nicky, Cole
Nigel	See Neil
Noel	French: 'birth day' or Christmas Day
Norman	Anglo-Saxon: 'north man' or Scandinavian
Oliver	Of confused origin, the best guess being a long-ago derivation from the

	Old Norse names Olaf or Olav. Abbr. Ollie, Nolly
Oscar	From the Old English Osgar = 'god spear'
Oswald	Old English: 'god power'. In use from the time of seventh-century St Oswald. Abbr. Ossie, Ozzy, Waldo
Owen	See Euan

Unisex names

What do Billie, Bobby, Beverly and Hilary have in common? They are all interchangeable names, used for both sexes. So are Evelyn, Noel, Ashley and, although rarely today, Cecil. Gill or Gil can be a boy's name or a girl's: the former shortened from Gilbert, the latter from Gilberta. Lyn is another example; the boy gets his from a shortened Jocelyn, and the girl from Rosalyn, Lynne, Lynette or Linda. Girls are also called George (from Georgina); Jo (from Josephine); Rae (from Raelene) Clem or Clemmy (from Clementine) and Percy (from Persephone). Confusing, isn't it?

Paddy	Familiar form of Patrick
Patrick	From the Latin *patricius* = nobleman. A primitive form of the name was taken to Ireland in the fifth century and it gradually spread from there. Abbr. Pat
Paul	From the Latin *paulus* = small. From its Biblical beginning the name spread throughout Europe and was used in England before the Normans

Percival	(Also Perceval, Percy) From the Norman surname originating in Percheval. Abbr. Perce
Peter	Greek: 'stone'; the spelling derives from the Latin Petrus. Hugely popularised by St Peter (to whom over 1000 English churches are dedicated)
Philip	(Also Phillip) Greek: 'lover of horses'. The name was spread by the Macedonians during their conquests, and became widespread, both as a surname and first name, in the Middle Ages. Abbr. Phil, Pip
Piers	A Norman form of Peter
Quentin	(Also Quinton) From the Latin *quinctus* = fifth
Ralph	Old Norse: 'counsel wolf'. From Radulf it became Ralf and finally Ralph
Randolph	(Also Randal) Anglo-Saxon: 'shield wolf'; was a pre-Conquest name. Abbr. Randy, Ranulf
Raymond	Old German: 'mighty counsel, protection'. It was introduced by the Normans. Abbr. Ray
Reginald	From the Teutonic Reginwald = 'mighty rule'. It changed to the Anglo-Saxon Regenweald and after the Normans combined with the French Reinald and later Reynaud to a range of names from Reynold and Ronald to Reinhold and Reginald. Abbr. Reg, Reggie
Rex	Latin: 'king'. In use only from the late nineteenth century
Richard	Anglo-Saxon: 'hard ruler'. Abbr. Dick, Rick, Ric

84

Robert	Old German: 'bright fame'. A good example of an Anglo-Saxon name, Hreodbeorht, merging with a Norman name, Robert, after 1066. Many variants have flourished, both as surnames (Robins, Robson, Dobson, Robertson, Robards, etc) and Christian names (Rob, Robbie, Bob, Bobby, Robin, Rab, Rupert)
Roderick	Old German: 'fame rule'. Abbr. Rod, Roddy, Rory
Rodney	From the Somerset surname based on the place-name Rodney Stoke. Abbr. Rod, Roddy
Roger	A combination of Anglo-Saxon Hrothgar and Norman Roger, the former meaning 'famous spear'
Roland	Old German: 'fame land'
Ronald	See Reginald. Ronald emerged as a Scottish form of Reynold. Abbr. Ron, Ronnie, Ranald

---

Rhyming Ronald

Pennsylvania poet Ronald Dell was so happy with his first name that he composed it into an acrostic rhyme:

R ed-eyed, fat, mean and hairy,
O rnery, growling, downright scary,
N ow that's my wife. Now here is me:
A jolly, handsome reverie,
L ovely, generous, kind and sweet,
D amnably humble from head to feet.

Rory	See Roderick
Ross	From the Scottish and Irish surname

Rowan	From the surnames Rowan and Rowland, after the Rowan tree. Probably of Old Norse origin
Roy	From the Gaelic *ruadh* = red, or red-haired. Was once a predominantly Scottish name
Rupert	See Robert, of which it is the Germanic version
Russell	From the French nickname *rouselle*, meaning red-haired. Abbr. Russ, Rusty
Ryan	From the Irish surname
Samuel	Hebrew: 'name of God'. The name of the great prophet, it did not catch on in England until the seventeenth century. Abbr. Sam, Sammy
Sandy	Short version of Alexander
Saul	Hebrew: 'asked for'. A predominantly Jewish name. Abbr. Sol, Solly
Scott	Originally a surname signifying a Scot
Seamus	Irish version of James
Sean	Irish version of the French Jean = John
Sebastian	Originally someone from the city of Sebastia, from the Greek *sevastos*, meaning 'venerable'. Abbr. Seb
Selwyn	Old English: 'house friend'
Shane	(Also Shaun) English versions of the Irish Sean
Sidney	(Also Sydney) An old English surname, being a contraction of Saint Denis. Abbr. Sid
Simon	A New Testament name derived from the Hebrew Shimeon, later Simeon. Very popular in the Middle Ages, it also spawned many surnames: Sim, Syme, Simmonds, Simpson, Simkins, etc. Abbr. Si

Sinclair	Contraction of Saint Clair in Normandy
Siôn	Welsh version of John
Solomon	Hebrew: 'man of peace'. A Biblical name and mostly a Jewish one, for surnames as well (Salaman, Salmon etc). Abbr. Sol, Solly
Spencer	Originally Old French, then an aristocratic surname
Stanley	From the Anglo-Saxon: 'stony field' and then an English surname. Abbr. Stan

Stephen

St Stephen was the world's first Christian martyr, which may account for Stephen's longevity as an internationally popular name. In a study of birth registrations over several centuries in England and Wales, Stephen proved to be the most popular first name, although only narrowly over Paul, William and John. The name derives from the Greek, meaning 'crowned'. Variants include Stephan, Stefan, Ystffan (Welsh version), Steven, Steve and Stevie

Steven	See Stephen
Stewart	(Also Stuart) Old English: 'steward' or household manager. From this occupation sprang the surname and ultimately the royal Scottish clan name. Used as a first name from the nineteenth century. Abbr. Stu, Stew
Ted	Short form of Theodore, sometimes Edward

Terence	From the Roman family name Terentius. Abbr. Terry, Tel, Tyrrel
Theodore	Greek: 'God's gift'. Abbr. Theo, Ted, Teddy
Thomas	Aramaic: 'twin'. Although popular because it was the name of an apostle, its use increased greatly after the murder of Archbishop of Canterbury Thomas à Becket in 1170. Abbr. Tom, Tommy, Tam
Timothy	Greek: 'honour God'. Abbr. Tim, Timmy
Toby	(And Tobias) Hebrew: 'God is good'. Toby is the English version of the Biblical Tobiah
Tom	See Thomas
Tony	See Anthony
Trevor	English version of the Welsh name Trefor, meaning 'large place'. Abbr. Trev
Tristram	(Also Tristan) Celtic: 'tumult'
Tudor	Welsh version of Theodore
Tyrone	Old Irish: From the county name meaning 'Owen's land'. Abbr. Ty
Vaughan	Old Welsh: 'little'. Originally a surname
Vernon	From a Norman place-name. Abbr. Vern
Victor	Latin: 'victor'. As a masculine version of Victoria, it became popular during the nineteenth century
Vincent	From the Latin *vincentius* = conquering
Wally	Short form of Walter or Wallace
Walter	From the Old German Waldhar, meaning 'rule folk' and introduced by the Normans although there was a

	similar Anglo-Saxon name, Wealdhere. Abbr. Wal, Wally, Walt, Wat
Warren	Old German: 'warrior' or 'defender'
Wayne	A recent reworking of the old English wainwright, or wagon maker
Wilfred	(Also Wilfrid) Anglo-Saxon: 'will peace'. Derives from the original name Wilfrith. Abbr. Wilf, Will
Will	Short version of William, Wilfred or Wilbur
William	From the Old German Willahelm, meaning 'will and helmet', it arrived in England, rather forcibly, with William the Conqueror. Since then a widespread surname (Willis, Wilson, Wilkinson, etc) and a first name. Abbr. Will, Bill, Billy, Willie
Winston	From the place-name near Cirencester, and closely identified with the Churchill family

Z names

While Zöe seems to have taken off as a girl's name, no parent appears to be keen on forenames for boys beginning with the last letter of the alphabet, like Zachary, Zane (remember Zane Grey, the writer of Westerns?), Zeke . . . there the list ends. So the holders of the world's last last names – Zachary Zzzra, Zeke ZZZpt and Zero ZZyzx – can rest easy.

Are You Properly Addressed?

Once upon a time it was easy. If you wanted to send a letter to the head of an organisation you simply wrote, 'Dear Sir'. Nowadays, with an increasing proportion of women running businesses, this just isn't acceptable and we have to write, 'Dear Sir or Madam' or 'Dear Madam or Sir'.

In these days of familiarity and equality fresh ambiguities are introduced. Say you receive a letter signed Gill Jones, or Lyn Smith; you fire back a reply to Mr Jones or Miss Smith only to discover that they are respectively Mrs Gillian Jones and Mr Jocelyn Smith.

So it is sometimes a relief to have the computer to blame. It blithely once addressed the Chief Fire Officer at the Lambeth headquarters of the London Fire Brigade as 'Dear Mr Albert Embankment'. Another gentleman, who unguardedly signed a letter with his name followed by MBE (Member of the Order of the British Empire), was forever after addressed as 'Mr Mbe'. A similar misfortune attended the correspondence between the brother of newspaper columnist Bernard Levin and the British Home Office; to add weight to an appeal on behalf of the family's Nigerian au pair, he added after his signature the letters of honour and professionalism to which he was entitled: OBE (Order of the British Empire), RDI (Royal Designer for Industry) and FSIA (Fellow of the Society of Industrial Artists). The Home Office reply began, 'Dear Mr Oberdifsia'.

A bank customer received a letter marked Private and Confidential addressed 'Dear Private Confidential'; while a former customer of the Bank of Ireland was sent a mailshot from the bank addressed, 'Dear Mr

'Hawkes Decd', expressing the hope that 'we can be of continued service to you in the future'.

The British aren't the only players in the *Are You Properly Addressed?* stakes. Recently the London booksellers Mowbray & Co Ltd replied to an enquiry from a Japanese customer, adding at the end, '. . . please ask for further details if necessary.' The following letter from the Japanese customer obediently began, 'Dear Father Details . . .'

How To Pronounce Those Difficult Names

In a few lines of verse about the Victorian poet Arthur Clough, the American language scholar Willard Espy demonstrates how easy it is to be led astray by a language in which four out of five words are not spelled the way they sound:

> I seldom rest beneath a bough
> To read the lines of Arthur Clough.
> I find his thoughts insipid, though
> Victorians loved Arthur Clough.
> Indeed, they could not get enough
> Of platitudes by Arthur Clough.
> I groan, I gulp, I snort, I cough
> When I must wade through Arthur Clough;
> And I am glad that I am through
> With this review of Arthur Clough.

So here we have bough as in pow, though as in snow, enough as in snuff, cough as in off and through as in few. Phew! Little wonder, then, that we often put our feet in our mouths when attempting to say somebody's name. Who, except her friends perhaps, would know that Jacintha is pronounced Jassinter? Or realise why Siobhan would reward you with a shrivelling glare if you pronounced her name other than Shivawn? It's all neatly sewn up in the delightful story about the crooked financier Horatio Bottomley who, giving his cloak and hat to Lord Cholmondeley's butler, said, 'Tell his Lordship that Mr Bumley would like to see him.'

Aaron	Air-un
Aesop	Ee-sop
Aloysius	Allo-wishus

Aneurin	An-eye-rin
Aquinas	Akw-eye-nas
Armand	Armon
Auberon	Ober-ron
Bach	Bahrk
Baudelaire	Bo-del-air
Beatrice	Bee-a-tris
Beauchamp	Bee-sham
Beaulieu	Bew-lee
Beethoven	Bay-toe-ven
Bethune	Bee-ton
Boccaccio	Bok-kart-cho
Botticelli	Botti-chellee
Brontë	Bron-tih
Brougham	Brew-um
Buccleugh	Buk-loo
Buchan	Buk-han
Buchanan	Bukkan-an
Calhoun	Kal-hoon
Candace, Candice	Kan-diss
Cellini	Chel-leen-ee
Cézanne	Say-zann
Charlemagne	Shar-le-man
Charlotte	Shar-lot
Cheops	Kee-ops
Chloë	Klo-ee
Clodagh	Klo-dar
Chopin	Sho-pahn
Cockburn	Ko-bern
Corot	Ko-ro
Correggio	Kor-red-jo
Dai	Die
Debussy	Deh-boo-see
Deidre	Dee-i-dree
Descartes	Day-karht
Désirée	Day-zeer-ray
Devereux	Dever-ooks
Dolores	Do-lor-rez
Donne	Dunn

Doré	Doh-ray
Duane	Dwain
Dumas	Doo-mar
Dylan	Dil-lun

The film producer SAM GOLDWYN was a master of the malapropism when it came to names. He once invited the British Foreign Secretary, Sir Samuel Hoare, to visit his MGM Studios in Hollywood. After the studio tour Goldwyn said goodbye to his guest, adding, 'And please give my regards to Lady W'.

Elöise	Ell-lo-eez
Emile	Ay-meel
Evelyn	Eev-lin
Farquhar	Fahr-kar or Far-kwar
Featherstone-haugh	Various families pronounce their name differently: Fether-stone-hoff, Fes-ton-hor, Feer-ston-hor, Fan-shor, and Fess-on-hay. Check first.
Flaubert	Flo-bare
Francesca	Fran-ches-ka
François	Fron-swar
Froude	Frood
Gascoigne	Gas-koyn
Gauguin	Go-gahn
Geraint	Gerrign't
Ghislaine	Geez-lan
Gluck	Glook
Goethe	Ger-tuh
Gough	Goff
Gounod	Goo-no
Haydn	Hide'n
Hegel	Hay-gell
Heine	Hine-ih

Hermione	Her-my-o-nee
Hywell	How-ell
Ifor	Eev-or
Inge	Ing
Irene	Eye-reen or Eye-reen-ee
Jacintha	Jass-inter
José	Ho-say
Juarez	Hwar-raz
Jules	Zhool
Knollys	Noles
Lachlan	Lok-lan
La Rochefoucauld	Lah-rorsh-foo-ko
Leighton	Lay-ton
Leila	Lay-lah
Levi	Leev-eye
Llewelyn	Kloo-ellin
Machiavelli	Mah-ki-arvelli
Maeterlinck	May-ter-lingk
Mainwaring	Mannering
Marat	Mar-ra
Maupassant	Mo-par-sarhn
Medici	Med-ee-chee
Mercator	Mer-kay-ter
Meyer	Mi-er
Meyrick	Merrick
Michelet	Meesh-leh
Michelle	M'shell
Millais	Mil-lay
Molière	Mo-lyair
Myfanwy	Muh-van-wee
Naomi	Nay-o-mee
Nkrumah	En-kroo-ma; as with similar Nigerian names, the N is pronounced 'En'
Pepys	Usually Peeps, but also Peppiss
Pericles	Perri-kleez
Phoebe	Fee-bee
Pierre	Pi-air
Poussin	Poo-sahn

Powys	Pow-iss
Proust	Proost
Ptolemy	Toll-e-mee
Puccini	Poot-chee-ni
Raquel	Rak-ell
Raoul	Row-ool
Renée	R'nay
Reuters	Roy-ters
Richelieu	Ree-sh-lehr
Rodin	Ro-dahn
Rousseau	Roo-so
Saint-Saëns	Sahn-Sahrns
St John	In some cases (St John Stevas) it is Sin-jun; in others (actress Jill Saint John) it is Saint-John
Sacheverell	Sash-ever-all
Salome	Sal-o-mee
Schopenhauer	Sho-pen-how-ah
Schuyler	Sky-ler
Seamus	Shay-mus
Sean	Shawn
Shankar	San-kar
Simone	See-mon
Sinead	Shin-aid
Siobhan	Shiv-awn
Synge	Sing
Titian	Tee-shun
Tollemache	Toll-mash
Trollope	Troll-up
Turgenev	Toor-gen-yef
Ulrike	Ull-rika
Vanbrugh	Van-bruh
Van Gogh	Van-Gokh
Vaughan	Vawn
Velasquez	Vel-lask-ehth
Wagner	Varg-nuh
Warwick	Wor-ik
Weber	Vay-ber
Wemyss	Weems

Yeats	Yayts
Yvette	Ee-vet
Yvonne	Ee-von
Zoë	Zo-ee

New Friends, New Neighbours, New Names

Over the past few decades, Britain has become increasingly multi-cultural. Along with different beliefs, lifestyles and appearances these recent arrivals have also brought with them new names. If, at a local meeting, you were introduced to the following, could you guess their country of origin from their given names? (Answers on next page):

1.	Ganesh	5.	Chukwama
2.	Cemal	6.	Radu
3.	Monique	7.	Rienke
4.	Khalid	8.	Andrzej

Six out of eight would be a reasonable score and would demonstrate that you have an above-average awareness of Britain's increasingly multi-ethnic society.

Fair enough, you may say, but how do you tell a person's nationality from his or her name with a degree of accuracy? The answer is that you probably can't, but here are a few rules of thumb that may point you in the right direction. Do not be afraid to ask, however; invariably, people are proud of the country of their birth and will welcome your polite enquiry.

MUSLIM NAMES Muslim names are not so much linked to a nationality, but to Islam; thus the owner of a Muslim name might come from Pakistan, Malaysia, Kuwait or Africa. Because these names have had to be transcribed from languages using different characters into our own alphabet, a certain amount of simplification has taken place. While this helps enormously, addressing someone with a Muslim name can still be tricky; a first name is often a title, like Mohammed, Syed or Allah, which can be dropped – it is the second or middle name that counts. Fairly common Muslim names include: (for females) Aisha, Azhar, Bushra, Farah, Karimah, Nadimah, Najmah, Nasimah or Naseema, Uzma and Yasmin; (for males) Abdullah, Akbar, Ali, Aziz, Bashir, Hanif, Hashim, Hussain, Khalid, Latif, Rafiq, Rashid, Salim, Sharif and Zahid.

Answers to Nationality Quiz
1. Hindu   2. Turkish   3. French   4. Muslim
5. Nigerian   6. Romanian   7. Dutch
8. Polish

HINDU NAMES Hindu naming is a complex business and most given names have some religious significance. Typical are these: (female) Aruna, Indira, Mohani, Rohini, Sumitra and Usha; (male) Anil, Ganesh, Kanti, Naresh, Rajesh, Ram and Vijay.

SIKH NAMES Ranjit Singh is a recognisable Sikh name because of the 'Singh', which indicates that the owner is a male; a female uses Kaur after her first name. A surname should follow but often doesn't, which is a bit annoying when you look in the telephone directory and find half a column of Singh A, another half-column of Singh B, and so on. The Sikhs would be doing themselves and everyone else a favour if they used their full given names which invariably serve both sexes and include Ajit, Amarjit, Avtar, Baljit, Daljit, Darshan, Fauja, Jarnail, Manjit, Mohan, Paramjit, Pritham, Rajinda, Ramindar, Ranjit, Salh, Sardar, Sohan and Surjit.

AFRICAN NAMES These are not easy, because in many of the former colonies, Ghana for instance, Joseph and Ignatius rub shoulders with Kofi and Kwame. In Nigeria, with a population half as big again as Britain's, there also exist over 200 ethnic and linguistic groups, so it's unreasonable to expect any clear name patterns. The A&O rule is a crude attempt at identification, and it goes like this: if a name looks and sounds like Akinyosoye, Akintara, Adekunle, Azikiwe, Ojukwu, Ojurongbe, Obasanjo or Ojimadu, there is a chance that the owner hails from Nigeria. There are also the 'day names': the result of an African tradition of naming children for the weekday on which they were born. This results in a number of very common given names: Kwadwo, Kwabena, Kwaku and Kwasi for boys, and Abena, Akua, Afua and Akosua for girls.

CHINESE NAMES The first thing to learn about these is that the surname comes first: Deng Xiaoping is really Mr Deng. The next thing is that Chinese given names are actually words with meanings, like strong, learned, ambitious, important, etc. The final thing is that in 1978 China adopted a new system for spelling Chinese names in the Roman alphabet, known as Pinyin. What makes Chinese confusing is that many names, like Peking, are still spelt that way instead of the phonetically accurate Beijing. A Chinese would have great difficulty in saying Chang with its hard 'ch', but none whatsoever with Zhang.

JAPANESE NAMES There can hardly be a home in Britain without a Japanese-named product in it, so the sound of Japanese isn't so strange to our ears any more. But we still lack familiarity with Japanese given names and surnames, and most people would say that they couldn't tell the difference between Japanese and Chinese. But it is really quite clear, as this selection of first names shows: (female) Akiko, Kyoko, Sakae, Sakura, Torao, Mami, Yoko and Yuko; (male) Akira, Eiji, Kazuo, Kentaro, Makoto, Minoru, Shingo, Takeshi and Toru.

Fractured names

You can have a lot of fun playing around with names. Fractured Names is a game invented by *New York Magazine* and is an established favourite with its readers. Here are some of the results:

MOUNTY PYTHON – Canadian policeman who always gets his snake

ELTON JOHN SMITH – Pop singer who frequents motels

MARY CASSETTE – Recording artist

J R R TOKEN – English fantasy writer whose tiny characters, the Habits, smoke dope and live in subways

SISSY SPACESICK – Fey astronaut stricken with *mal de air*

JOHN PAUL SIMON – Songwriter, critic, and pontiff

CHRISTOPHER ROBIN HOOD – Legendary outlaw who robbed the rich to give to the Pooh

LOUISA MAE WEST – Author of *Big Women*

MICHAEL CAINE AND ABEL – Precursor to Peter, Paul and Mary

LUCKY LUCIANO PAVAROTTI – Gangster who 'sang' to the Feds

POPE JOHN PAUL GEORGE RINGO – Pontiff who claimed to be more popular than Jesus

BALA LUGOSI – Welsh vampire

SHAH NA NA – Anti-government group in Iran

JOYCE CAROL OATS – Author of *Life With Fodder*

FRANCIS BAKIN' – Reputed author of *Is Paris Burnin'?*

OLIVIA NEWTON JOHN DONNE – Pop singer who had the big hit, *Let's Get Metaphysical*

SIR WALTER SCOTT JOPLIN – Composed *Ivanhoe Rag*

PINK FLOYD WRIGHT – Surrealist architect

Nicknames

A young girl was once asked by her teacher what, in her home, her mother called her father. 'She doesn't call him anything,' the girl replied. 'She likes him.'

In fact it is almost certain that her mother would call her father by perhaps several names in addition to his given names, even if they were pet names like Dear, Darling, Lover or (shudder) Snookums. At work, if his name was Clark, he might be called Nobby; if he was bald, Curly; if he was aggressive or abrasive, 'The Butcher'. All these additional names are known as nicknames.

Nicknames are generated for a number of reasons. Many are friendly, alliterative handles, like 'Stainless' Steele, or 'Red' Fox. Some are mildly derogatory, like 'Piggy' Taylor, or 'Two Dinners' (for someone who overeats). Others are purely descriptive, like Ginger and Lofty. And still others are traditionally linked with certain surnames, like Chalky White, Tug Wilson and Spud Murphy.

Then there are those nicknames that have become household names and, in some cases, immediately and internationally recognised, often after the lapse of many years. What follows is a selected list of such names, most of which you probably know, and some that, while you know the nickname, you may not recognise the person behind it.

Adrian Quist Former Australian tennis champion but now applied to someone who is inebriated

America's Sweetheart Film actress Mary Pickford (1893–1979)

Beaver, The Newspaper owner Lord Beaverbrook (1879–1964)

Bloody Mary Queen Mary, the daughter of Henry VIII

Bobby A British policeman, after Sir Robert Peel who created the London Police Force in 1830

Boney Napoleon Bonaparte

Brown Bomber American world heavyweight boxing champion, Joe Louis

Butcher of Broadway New York theatre critic Alexander Woolcott

Scarface American gangster Alphonse Capone (1899–1947)

Dizzy British Prime Minister Benjamin Disraeli

Don, The Australian cricketer Donald Bradman

G O M 'Grand Old Man' – British Prime Minister William Ewart Gladstone (1809–1898)

Iron Duke The Duke of Wellington

Iron Lady British Prime Minister Margaret Thatcher

Ike Former Us President General Dwight Eisenhower

Lady with the Lamp Florence Nightingale, hospital reformer

Manassa Mauler Heavyweight boxing champion Jack Dempsey

Merry Monarch King Charles II

Mr Five Per Cent British financier and oil millionaire Calouste Sarkis Gulbenkian (1869–1955)

Nosey Parker Dr Matthew Parker, Archbishop of Canterbury (1504–1575)

Old Blood and Guts World War II general George S Patton

Old Groaner Singer Frank Sinatra

Our Gracie English Singer Gracie Fields (1898–1979). Not to be confused with **Our Glad**, Australian singer Gladys Moncrieff (d 1976)

Phyllis and Sharon Reportedly the nicknames used by pop stars Rod Stewart and Elton John for each other

Plum Short for Pelham, and used for both the humorist Pelham Grenville Wodehouse and the cricketer Pelham Francis Warner

Ranji Cricketer Kumar Shri Ranjitsinhji

Red Baron German World War I ace pilot Manfred Freiherr von Richthofen (1892–1918)

Red Dean Dr Hewlett Johnson, Dean of Canterbury

Rockhampton Rocket Australian tennis star Rod Laver

Satchmo Jazz trumpeter Louis Armstrong (1900–1971)

Silly Billy William Frederick, Duke of Gloucester

Stonewall Jackson US Civil War General Thomas Jackson

Sunny Jim Former British Prime Minister James Callaghan

Supermac Former Prime Minister Harold Macmillan

Swedish Nightingale English singer Jenny Lind (1820–1887)

Tarzan Conservative cabinet minister Michael Heseltine

Teflon Don American mafia boss John Gotti

Thunderer, The Editorial writer Edward Sterling (1773–1847) whose nickname was eventually transferred to his employer, *The Times*

Tommy Nickname for British soldiers, after the specimen name Thomas Atkins (the British equivalent of the American Joe Doe) was used on Army sign-up forms

Tom Thumb The American dwarf Charles Stratton (1838–1883)

Trickie Dickie Former US President Richard Nixon

Twiggy English fashion model and actress Lesley Hornby

Uncle Joe Soviet dictator Josef Stalin (1879–1953)

Virgin Queen Queen Elizabeth I, who died childless

Wedgie Former Labour minister Anthony Wedgwood Benn

Welsh Windbag British Labour leader Neil Kinnock

Welsh Wizard Former British Prime Minister David Lloyd George (1863–1945)

Winnie British wartime Prime Minister Sir Winston Churchill

Wizard Dribbler English soccer captain Sir Stanley
  Matthews

A Word About Long Words About Names

The Greek word for name is *onoma*, and from this spring most of the words about names.

The study of names is called *onomastics* or sometimes *onomatology*. An onomatist is a rarely used word for a student of names; more often we hear of an *onomatomaniac*, which describes a person who is obsessed with names, words and the sound of words. If this *onomatomaniac* compiles a list of names it is called an *onomasticon*, which sounds vaguely threatening.

If a name is based on a person's father or grandfather (Robertson = son of Robert; O'Brien = grandson of Brien, etc) it is called a *patronymic*; if a name derives from the mother's side it is a *matronymic*. This mostly applies to given names, as when a name like Grace is used successively by the grandmother, mother and daughter.

An *anonym* is, as the 'anon' suggests, someone who is either unknown or doesn't want to be known. While that person remains *anonymous*, a person who is known by many names (aka's) is *polyonymous*. When a person uses a name other than his own, in other words a fictitious name, that name is called a *pseudonym*; but if the name of another person is deliberately used to deceive it is an *allonym*.

We use *eponyms* every day, often without realising it, like teddy bear, wellies, leotard, camellia and sandwich. An *eponym* is the person after whom these things are named; for the eponyms of the above, see the list at the end of this book.

Finally, when you call someone a 'Jezebel' or a 'Casanova' or a 'little Hitler', you are indulging in *antonomasia*.

Changing Names

Many people change their names. The question is, why? Although Britain is a far cry from Korea, where there are only about three surnames, most of us will have at least one namesake, probably a dozen – that is, other people with exactly the same surname and given names. Recently, a newspaper asked its readers if they had a famous namesake, and was deluged with letters from William Shakespeare, Julie Andrews, Elizabeth Taylor, Davy Crockett, Steve McQueen and thousands more. Yet the temptation or need to change our names happens very rarely.

Of course, we make allowances for entertainers, and in any case the practice of inventing new names for actors and actresses is as old as Hollywood. Decades ago they changed the name of a promising actress named Lucille Le Sueur to Joan Crawford; today they would be just as likely to change the ordinary Joan Crawford to the more exotic Lucille Le Sueur. One can easily see the reasons for changing Robert Zimmerman to Bob Dylan, Paul Gadd to Gary Glitter, Bernard Jewry to Alvin Stardust and Bernard Schwartz to Tony Curtis. But it still comes as quite a surprise to learn that Morecambe and Wise were really Bartholomew and Wiseman.

Then there are those people with unfortunate names, or names which are difficult to spell or pronounce, usually belonging to immigrant families. The actor Walter Matthau made a smart move when he changed his surname from Matuschanskayasky, as did Dirk Bogarde, from Derek Van den Bogaerde. The source of some of these new names is intriguing, too; when the father of former union leader Ian Mikardo arrived at Dover, the first thing he spotted was a poster advertising the Gilbert and Sullivan comic opera, so that became their future name. It is also interesting that during the process of changing his name from Jan Hoch to Robert Maxwell, the late publisher was conning people under the name Jan du Maurier, chosen from a then fashionable brand of cigarette.

Another reason for name changing is expediency. If your name was Fred Chatterley and you were about to be offered a knighthood, you might reasonably expect some pressure from your wife to change the family name to Checkersly or Battersby or something like that. During World War I, with feelings against the Germans running high in Britain, the Royal Family found it most expedient to change the family name from Wettin – Grandfather Prince Albert was Prince Wettin of Saxe-Coburg-Gotha, and how German can you get? – to Windsor, which it remains today.

Pseudonyms – or *noms de plume*, they are the same – are a form of name change, customarily used by writers, but they are superficial and transient by comparison with the real thing. They can be discarded when their usefulness is over, and their owners always retain their original names.

Although it is not difficult to change your name in Britain, the US and most countries, few of us go through with the process without good reason. It is strange, therefore, that name changing is made so difficult in France, where only a few hundred citizens each year are able to do so. The restriction dates from the Revolution, and only under special circumstances will the Ministry of Justice authorise a change. Among those who were privileged to do so were a Hitler, a Frankenstein, a Dr Sida (Sida is French for Aids) and a Mme Hrynczyzsyn.

Some People Who Changed Their Names

The name on the left is the name by which we now know the person; that on the right is the original name.

Spiro Agnew	Spiro Anagnostopoulos
Dave Allen	David O'Mahoney
Julie Andrews	Julia Elizabeth Wells
Fred Astaire	Frederick Austerlitz
Charles Aznavour	Charles Aznavurgan
Gene Barry	Eugene Klass
Lionel Bart	Lionel Begleiter
Dirk Bogarde	Derek Van den Bogaerde
Marc Bolan	Mark Feld
David Bowie	David Hayward-Jones
Katie Boyle	Caterina di Francavilla
Charles Bronson	Charles Buchinsky
Mel Brooks	Melvin Kaminsky
Richard Burton	Richard Walter Jenkins
Marti Caine	Lynda Crapper
Michael Caine	Maurice Micklewhite
Maria Callas	Cecilia Kalegeropoulos
Lewis Carroll	Charles Lutwidge Dodgson
Joseph Conrad	Theodore Korzeniowski
Elvis Costello	Declan McManus
Joan Crawford	Lucille Le Sueur
Michael Crawford	Michael Dumble-Smith
Doris Day	Doris Kappelhoff
Diana Dors	Diana Fluck
Kirk Douglas	Issur Demsky
Bob Dylan	Robert Zimmerman
George Eliot	Mary Ann Evans
David Essex	David Cook

Kenny Everett	Maurice Cole
Adam Faith	Terence Nelhams
Georgie Fame	Clive Powell
Gracie Fields	Grace Stansfield
W C Fields	William Claude Dukinfield
Margot Fonteyn	Margaret Hookham
Connie Francis	Constance Franconero
Greta Garbo	Greta Gustafsson
Ava Gardner	Lucy Johnson
Judy Garland	Frances Ethel Gumm
George Gershwin	Jacob Gershvin
Gary Glitter	Paul Gadd
Samuel Goldwyn	Samuel Goldfish
Cary Grant	Archibald Leach
Larry Grayson	William White
David Hamilton	David Pilditch
Lawrence Harvey	Larushka Skikne
O Henry	William Sydney Porter
Audrey Hepburn	Edda Hepburn van Heemstra
Bob Hope	Leslie Hope
Frankie Howerd	Francis Howard
Rock Hudson	Roy Fitzgerald
Engelbert Humperdinck	Arnold George Dorsey
Betty Hutton	Elizabeth Thornburg
Elton John	Reginald Dwight
Al Jolson	Asa Yoelson
Boris Karloff	William Pratt
Danny Kaye	David Kaminsky
Alexander Korda	Sandro Kellner
Frankie Laine	Frank Lo Vecchio
Michael Landon	Eugene Orowitz
Cleo Laine	Clementine Campbell
Mario Lanza	Alfredo Cococozza
Danny La Rue	Daniel Carroll

John Le Carré	David Cornwell
Bruce Lee	Lee Yuen Kam
Lenin	Vladimir Ilyich Ulanov
Rula Lenska	Roza-Maria Lubienska
Lulu	Marie Lawrie
Vera Lynn	Vera Welch
Hugh MacDiarmid	Christopher Grieve
Karl Malden	Malden Sekulovitch
Jayne Mansfield	Vera Jayne Palmer
Dean Martin	Dino Crocetti
Marx Brothers	Julius, Leonard, Arthur, Milton and Herbert Marx
Walter Matthau	Walter Matuschanskayasky
Robert Maxwell	Jan Hoch
Dame Nellie Melba	Helen Armstrong
Guy Mitchell	Al Cernick
Marilyn Monroe	Norma Jean Baker
Morecambe and Wise	Eric Bartholomew and Ernest Wiseman
Muhammad Ali	Cassius Marcellus Clay
Anna Neagle	Marjorie Robinson
Ivor Novello	Ifor Davies
George Orwell	Eric Arthur Blair
Gilbert O'Sullivan	Raymond O'Sullivan
Pelé	Edson Arantes do Nascimento
Edith Piaf	Edith Gassion
P J Proby	James Smith
Ellery Queen	Two cousins, Frederic Dannay and Manfred Lee, used this pseudonym
Debbie Reynolds	Mary Frances Reynolds
Cliff Richard	Harold Webb
Sugar Ray Robinson	Walker Smith
Ginger Rogers	Virginia McMath

Roy Rogers	Leonard Slye
Mickey Rooney	Michael McGuire
Leo Sayer	Gerard Sayer
Omar Sharif	Michel Shalhoub
Martin Sheen	Ramon Estevez
Beverly Sills	Beverly Silvermann
Nina Simone	Eunice Waymon
Penny Singleton	Dorothy McNulty
Alvin Stardust	Bernard Jewry
Ringo Starr	Richard Starkey
Tommy Steele	Thomas Hicks
Terry Thomas	Thomas Terry Hoar-Stevens
Mark Twain	Samuel Clemens
Twiggy	Lesley Hornby
Conway Twitty	Harold Jenkins
Frankie Vaughan	Frank Abelsohn
Sid Vicious	John Beverley
Max Wall	Maxwell Lorimer
Edgar Wallace	Richard Edgar
Andy Warhol	Andy Warhola
John Wayne	Marion Morrison
Rebecca West	Cicily Isabel Fairfield
Barbara Windsor	Barbara Deeks
Stevie Wonder	Stephen Judkins
Natalie Wood	Natasha Gurdin
Tammy Wynette	Wynette Pugh
Malcolm X	Malcolm Little
Michael X	Michael de Freitas

How Persons Become Words

Among the most generous contributors to our stock of words have been the several thousand persons who have given their names to objects, products, theories, diseases, plants, organisations and activities.

The names of these lucky people have not only been enshrined in the language as everyday words, but they have also been awarded a name; a person after whom something is named is called an *eponym*.

There are many thousands of them alive and well today – not the persons, but the words. The infamous Marquis de Sade (sadism) and the Fourth Earl of Sandwich (sandwich) expired some time ago, but their names will be remembered for ever.

What follows is a mere taste of this fascinating source of our words; moreover it is restricted to eponyms that are or were real people and not literary (a 'Jekyll and Hyde') or mythological ('Junoesque') characters or place-names (a 'balaclava'). To explore further, consult the Reading Guide at the end of this book.

America	Named after the Italian explorer Amerigo Vespucci (1454–1512)
Aubrietia	This attractive purple-flowered plant was named after the flower painter Claude Aubriel
Bartlett pear	Enoch Bartlett (1779–1860) first imported them into America
Begonia	Named after the amateur naturalist Michel Bégon (1638–1710) who found it in Santo Domingo
Belisha Beacon	Introduced in the 1930s by the then Minister of Transport, Sir Leslie Hore-Belisha

Big Ben	In honour of Sir Benjamin Hall who was Chief Commissioner of Works in the 1850s
Biro	The child of its Hungarian inventor, Lázló Biró
Bloomers	An undergarment for women introduced by Amelia Bloomer in Massachusetts in 1851
Bowie knife	Named after American Colonel Jim Bowie
Boycott	One of the first to suffer from this form of ostracizing was Charles Cunningham Boycott (1832–97). His great-great-niece, Rosie Boycott, has herself written a small dictionary of eponyms
Braille	This system of printing books for the blind was invented by Louis Braille (1809–52)
Buddleia	A shrub named after the seventeenth-century Rev Adam Buddle
Camellia	After the seventeenth-century Jesuit priest George Kamel
Cardigan	Named after the 7th Earl of Cardigan, who led the Charge of the Light Brigade in 1854
Casanova	After the amorous Italian Giovanni Casanova
Celsius	Anders Celsius developed this temperature scale in Sweden in 1742
Chauvinism	From the ultra-loyal French soldier Nicolas Chauvin
Crap	*Not* an eponym (popularly supposed to be derived from the London sanitary engineer Sir Thomas Crapper) but after the Latin *crapula*

Cruft's	Named after the organiser of the first dog show, Charles Cruft
Curie	This measure of radiation is named after the Nobel Prize-winner Marie Curie (1867–1934)
Dahlia	In honour of the Swedish botanist Anders Dahl
Darwinism	After the naturalist Charles Darwin (1809–82)
Davis Cup	In honour of American sportsman Dwight Davis who donated the trophy
Diesel	The inventor of the engine that bears his name was the German engineer Rudolph Diesel
Doberman	Its first breeder was Ludwig Doberman
Douglas Fir	After Scottish botanist David Douglas
Dow-Jones	This NYSE index of share prices is named after two late nineteenth-century financial analysts, Charles Dow and Edward D Jones
Down's Syndrome	Dr John Langdon-Down first described the symptoms of this defect in 1866
Eggs Benedict	After the creator, Samuel Benedict, in 1894
Eiffel Tower	The designer was Alexandre Eiffel (1832–1923)
Elgin Marbles	The statuary removed from the Parthenon in Athens by the Earl of Elgin (1766–1841)
Fahrenheit	The temperature scale (32–212 degrees) invented by Gabriel Fahrenheit (1686–1736)
Ferris Wheel	After the American George Washington Ferris

Forsythia	Shrub named after Scottish botanist William Forsyth (1737–1804)
Freesia	After the nineteenth-century German Dr Friedrich Freese
Freudian slip	After Sigmund Freud, father of psychoanalysis
Gallup Poll	This device for assessing public opinion was developed by the US statistician George Gallup
Gardenia	After the eighteenth-century botanist Dr Alexander Garden
Gerrymander	This term for electoral skullduggery is named after Massachusetts governor Elbridge Gerry (1744–1814)
Gibson Girl	After the luscious pen drawings of girls by nineteenth-century American artist Charles Dana Gibson
Gladstone bag	After British Prime Minister W E Gladstone
Goldwynism	A malapropism, typical of those dropped by the film producer Sam Goldwyn
Gordon Bennett	A euphemistic expression for 'God!' after the owner of the *New York Herald*, Gordon Bennett
Granny Smith	Apple named after Australian horticulturalist Granny Maria Smith
Guillotine	First used in 1792, it was promoted as a merciful decapitator by Dr Joseph Guillotin
Hansard	Named after the Hansard family of printers for the House of Commons

Heath Robinson	A rickety, improbable construction that actually works is called thus after the artist William Heath Robinson (1872–1944) who specialised in drawing them. His American equivalent is Rube Goldberg (1883–1970)
Hitler	A heartless, dictatorial 'little Hitler' is of course named after Adolf Hitler (1889–1945), one-time dictator of Germany
Hobson's choice	From seventeenth-century stable owner Thomas Hobson who offered his customers no choice at all for riding horses
Hooligan	After Irish roughneck Patrick Hooligan
Hoover	American William Henry Hoover was the cleaning machine's first salesman, then the owner
Hoyle	The phrase 'according to Hoyle' derives from seventeenth-century Edmund Hoyle, who compiled the rules for chess, whist, backgammon and other games
Jack Russell	A lively breed of hunting dog named after the West Country Revd Jack Russell (1795–1883)
Jacuzzi	After its Italian inventor Candido Jacuzzi
JCB	After its manufacturer, Joseph Cyril Bamford
John Hancock	From the ostentatious signature of John Hancock on the original American Declaration of Independence
Kafkaesque	The writings of Franz Kafka

	(1883–1924) are responsible for this adjective of isolation, fear and helplessness
Knickerbockers	From the pseudonym of writer Washington Irving
Leotard	After French acrobat Jules Leotard (1842–70)
Levis	From San Francisco clothing dealer Levi Strauss (1830–1902)
Lindy hop	A dance honouring Charles Lindbergh's flight across the Atlantic in 1927
Linnaean	After eighteenth-century Swedish botanist Carl Linnaeus
Listerine	After English surgeon Sir Joseph Lister
Loganberry	Named after its creator, American James Logan
McCarthyism	After the communist witchhunter Senator Joseph McCarthy (1909–57)
Mach 2.2	After physicist Ernst Mach, a measurement of speed in terms of the speed of sound; Concorde flies at about Mach 2.2
Mackintosh	After nineteenth-century Scottish chemist Charles Mackintosh
Magnolia	Shrub named after seventeenth-century French botanist Pierre Magnol
Malthusian	After the doom-laden population theories of Thomas Malthus (1766–1834)
Martinet	After French Army disciplinarian Jean Martinet
Marxism	The social theories of German Karl Marx
Masochism	This name for experiencing

119

	pleasure from self-inflicted pain comes from the writings of Leopold von Sacher-Masoch (1836–95)
Maverick	After frontiersman Samuel Maverick (1803–70)
Melba toast	After Australian opera star Dame Nellie Melba
Mesmerize	After Austrian hypnotist Dr Franz Mesmer
Molotov Cocktail	Bottles of flaming petrol first used against Russian tanks and Comrade Molotov
Montessori	The educational methods of Maria Montessori
Moog	One of the first (1965) musical synthesisers developed by American Robert Moog
Morse Code	After its inventor Samuel Morse (1791–1872)
Ned Kelly	To be 'as game as Ned Kelly', ie fatally foolhardy, is to imitate the nineteenth-century Australian bushranger Ned Kelly
Negus	A wine drink supposedly invented by eighteenth-century English Colonel Francis Negus
Nissen Hut	After Lt-Col Peter Nissen (1871–1930)
Nobel Prize	Endowed by Swedish chemist and inventor of dynamite, Alfred Nobel (1833–96)
Nosey Parker	After Dr Matthew Parker (1504–1575), Archbishop of Canterbury
Ohm	Unit of electrical resistance named after physicist George Ohm (1787–1854)

Orwellian	After English writer George Orwell (1903–50)
Pap test	Developed by George Papanicolaou (1883–1962)
Parkinson's disease	First described by English physician Dr James Parkinson (1755–1824)
Parkinson's law	After comic writer C Northcote Parkinson
Pasteurize	A process invented by French bacteriologist Louis Pasteur (1822–95)
Pavlova	The rich meringue cake made in honour of the Russian ballerina Anna Pavlova (1885–1931)
Pavlovian	A response to stimulus developed by Russian physiologist Ivan Pavlov (1849–1936)
Peach Melba	Favourite dessert of Australian diva Dame Nellie Melba
Pinchbeck	Imitation gold alloy named after eighteenth-century watchmaker and jeweller Christopher Pinchbeck
Plimsoll line	Safety loading line on ships named after Samuel Plimsoll (1824–98)
Plimsolls	Originally canvas shoes with a rubber upper that looked like a Plimsoll line (see above)
Pulitzer Prize	Given by the estate of New York newspaper owner Joseph Pulitzer (1847–1911)
Pullman coach	Inventor was American George Pullman (1831–97)
Quisling	After Norwegian World War II collaborator with the Germans, Vidkun Quisling
Rachmanism	Unscrupulous landlord tactics

	introduced by London property tycoon Perec Rachman (1920–62)
Raglan	After Crimean commander Lord Raglan (1788–1855)
Reuters	After newsagency founder Paul Reuter (1816–99)
Richter Scale	Measurement of effect of earthquakes devised by seismologist Charles Richter (1900–85)
Rorschach test	The 'interpretation of inkblot' test devised by Swiss psychiatrist Hermann Rorschach in 1921
Salk vaccine	Polio vaccine named after Dr Jonas Salk
Sadism	From the writings of the Marquis de Sade
Sandwich	Convenient snack invented by inveterate gambler the Fourth Earl of Sandwich (1718–92)
Sanforized	After American scientist Sandford Cluett
Saxophone	Blame Belgian Adolphe Sax (1814–94)
Sequoia	Giant tree species named after Cherokee Indian linguist Sequoya in the early nineteenth century
Shavian	Anything to do with the works of Irish writer and dramatist George Bernard Shaw (1856–1950)
Shrapnel	Inventor was British Army artillery officer Henry Shrapnel (1761–1842)
Silhouette	After eighteenth-century French finance minister Étienne de Silhouette
Sousaphone	Developed by American brass

	band composer John Philip Sousa (1854–1932)
Spode	Porcelain made by Josiah Spode (1754–1827)
Spoonerism	Hilarious transposed slips of the tongue made famous by the Rev William Archibald Spooner
Stetson	After American hatter John Stetson (1830–1906)
Stradivarius	Violins made by Antonio Stradivari (1644–1737) and his sons Francesco and Omobono
Teddy Bear	After US President Theodore Roosevelt
Thatcherism	Ultra-Conservative free market policies of British Prime Minister Margaret Thatcher
Volt	After Italian physicist Alessandro Volta (1745–1827) who also invented the battery
Wagnerian	Histrionic musical drama of the kind composed by Wilhelm Richard Wagner (1813–83)
Wassermann Test	Diagnostic test for the presence of syphilis, developed by August von Wassermann (1866–1925)
Watt	Unit of electrical power invented by Scottish engineer James Watt (1736–1819)
Wellie	Originally a wellington boot named after the first Duke of Wellington (1769–1852)
Winchester	The rifle first manufactured by Oliver Winchester (1810–80) in Connecticut
Wisteria	Climbing plant named after Dr Caspar Wistar
Yale lock	Invented by nineteenth-century American locksmith Linus Yale

Zinnia   Named after eighteenth-century
German botanist Johann Zinn

Reading Guide

Surnames

A Dictionary of Surnames – Patrick Hanks and Flavia
    Hodges, Oxford University Press, 1988
A Dictionary of English and Welsh Surnames – Charles
    Bardsley, Genealogical Publishing Co
Dictionary of British Surnames – P H Reaney,
    Routledge & Kegan Paul, 1957
Discovering Surnames – J W Freeman, Shire
    Publications Ltd, 1973

Given names

Dictionary of First Names – Julia Cresswell,
    Bloomsbury, 1990
Discovering Christian Names – S M Jarvis, Shire
    Publications Ltd, 1986
Oxford Dictionary of English Christian Names –
    E G Withycombe, Oxford University Press, 1990
New Book of First Names – Michèle Brown, Corgi
    Books, 1991

Pronunciation

Pronouncing Dictionary of British Names –
    G M Miller, Oxford University Press, 1971

Nicknames

Nicknames – Vernon Noble, Hamish Hamilton, 1976

Changing names

Naming Names – Adrian Room, Routledge & Kegan
    Paul, 1981

Eponyms

Batty, Bloomers and Boycott – Rosie Boycott,
    Hutchinson, 1982
Dictionary of Eponyms – Martin Manser, Sphere
    Books

Thou Improper, Thou Uncommon Noun – Willard
Espy, Clarkson Potter, New York, 1978

General

The Guinness Book of Names – Leslie Dunkling,
Guinness Publishing, 1991

A Full List of Titles Available from Mandarin in this series

While every effort is made to keep prices low, it is sometimes necessary to increase prices at short notice. Mandarin Paperbacks reserves the right to show new retail prices on covers which may differ from those previously advertised in the text or elsewhere.

The prices shown below were correct at the time of going to press.

☐	7493 1519 9	**Word Bank**	Graham King	£2.99
☐	7493 1520 2	**Good Grammar in One Hour**	Graham King	£2.99
☐	7493 1521 0	**Crisp Clear Writing in One Hour**	Graham King	£2.99
☐	7493 1522 9	**Word Check**	Graham King	£2.99
☐	7493 1523 7	**The Secrets of Speed Reading**	Graham King	£2.99
☐	7493 1524 5	**The Name Book**	Graham King	£2.99
☐	7493 1525 3	**Spell Check**	Graham King	£2.99
☐	7493 1526 1	**Guide to Word Play & Word Games**	Graham King	£2.99

All these books are available at your bookshop or newsagent, or can be ordered direct from the publisher. Just tick the titles you want and fill in the form below.

Mandarin Paperbacks, Cash Sales Department, PO Box 11, Falmouth, Cornwall TR10 9EN.

Please send cheque or postal order, no currency, for purchase price quoted and allow the following for postage and packing:

UK including BFPO	£1.00 for the first book, 50p for the second and 30p for each additional book ordered to a maximum charge of £3.00.
Overseas including Eire	£2 for the first book, £1.00 for the second and 50p for each additional book thereafter.

NAME (Block letters) ....

ADDRESS ....

....

☐ I enclose my remittance for ....

☐ I wish to pay by Access/Visa Card Number

Expiry Date